Nordic Fund for Technology and Industrial Development
The Final Report from the NOR-LMT Project

LAYER MANUFACTURING
- A Tool for Reduction of Product Lead Time -

Edited by
Professor Øyvind Bjørke
NTNU-SINTEF, Trondheim

TAPIR PUBLISHERS
TRONDHEIM - NORWAY

© TAPIR Publishers, 1996

ISBN 82-519-1224-5

Printed by Tapir
Binding: Sandnes Bokbinderi A/S

PREFACE

This book represents a part of the final documentation of the project: "Layer Manufacturing as a Tool for Reduction of Product Lead Time" called NOR-LMT, founded by Nordic Fund for Technology and Industrial Development, the national research councils in the four countries, and industry.

The NOR-LMT project was designed in order to adapt Layer Manufacturing Technology (LMT) to industrial use, and to transfer the technology to the Nordic industry. This implies to develop design procedures, to adapt the different processes to cost efficient use, and to promote industry to take the new and promising technology into practical use.

It has been a pleasure for the Project Management Board to experience the enthusiasm shown by the 32 industrial partners who have contributed to the project. We would cordially thank of them for their contributions. Without their contribution the project could not have reached the good results as done. We also thank them for the financial support, counting for 50 % of the total budget. Further, we will sincerely thank The Nordic Fund for Technology and Industrial Development and the Research Councils in the four countries for their financial support, and for the great interest their officers have shown during the project period.

Finally, we would like to honour those who have contributed to this book:

- Bent Mieritz, DTI, Denmark
- Veli-Matti Tiainen, University of Helsinki, Juhani Seppanen and Jukka Tuomi, HUT/Lahti Centre, Andre Dolenc, HUT, Finland
- Nils Aksel Ruud and Øyvind Bjørke, Norway
- Bernt Holmer and Urban Harrison, IVF, Bernt Øquist, KOINOR, Sweden

The contributors of the examples in chapter 8 are mentioned in connection with their contribution.

CONTENTS

1 THE PROJECT   1
   1.1 BACKGROUND   1
   1.2 LAYER MANUFACTURING   2
   1.3 OVERALL GOAL   3
   1.4 PARTNERS   3
   1.5 WORK PROGRAM   5
      1.5.1 Work package 1: Design methodology   5
      1.5.2 Work package 2: Use of Layer Manufacturing in Casting   6
      1.5.3 Work package 3: 3D digitising and LMT in combination   7
      1.5.4 Work package 4: A feasibility study of computer   8
      1.5.5 Work package 5: Establish ISDN networks   8
      1.5.6 Work package 6: Technology transfer and networks for LMT   9

2. SUMMARY OF RESULTS   11
   2.1 LMT MACHINES IN THE NORDIC COUNTRIES   11
   2.2 GENERAL BENEFITS   13
      2.2.1 Application Areas   13
      2.2.2 Increased Know-how   15
   2.3 MAJOR RESULTS   15
      2.3.1 Design Methodology   15
      2.3.2 LMT in Casting   15
      2.3.3 3D Digitising and LMT in Combination   16
      2.3.4 Computer Aided Process Planning for LMT Processes   16
      2.3.5 High Speed Communication   16
      2.3.6 Technology Transfer   16

3 PROGRESS IN THE FIELD OF LMT   17
   3.1 PUBLISHED NEW PROCESSES   19
      3.1.1 Sanders Prototype Inc.   19

3.1.2 BPM Technologies Inc.	21
3.2 MATERIAL DEVELOPMENT	23
3.2.1 Metals	24
3.2.2 Other new RP-materials	27
3.3 FLOOD OF NEW MANUFACTURERS, SOFTWARE	27
3.4 MAJOR RESEARCH DIRECTIONS	30
3.4.1 Development of existing systems	31
3.4.2 New approaches and horizons	37
3.5 REFERENCES	40
4 DESIGN METHODOLOGY	**45**
4.1 INTRODUCTION	45
4.2 CHANGING REQUIREMENTS IN PRODUCT DEVELOPMENT	46
4.2.1 Changed Requirements for the Manufacturing Industry	46
4.2.2 Influence of RTP on Competition Parameters	49
4.3 HOW TO USE RPT?	50
4.3.1 Phases of a Product Development Process	50
4.3.2 Models	55
4.3.3 Models in Product Development	56
4.3.4 Classes of Models and Prototypes	62
5 LMT IN CASTING	**71**
5.1 INTRODUCTION	71
5.2 SAND CASTING	73
5.2.1 The Sand Casting Process	74
5.2.2 Different Ways of Combining FFF With Sand Casting	76
5.3 PLASTER CASTING	79
5.4 LOST WAX AND LOST FFF CASTING	79
5.4.1 The lost wax process	80
5.4.2 Different Methods of Combining FFF With Lost Wax Casting	80
5.5 PLASTIC INJECTION MOULDING	83
5.5.1 Test 1, Synthetic Design Element 1	84
5.5.2 Test 2, Synthetic Design Element 2	84
5.5.3 Test 3, Extractor for Print Boards	86
5.5.4 Test 4, Lamp Brightness Control Wheel	86
5.5.5 Test 5, Telephone Cover	87
5.6 EXAMPLES	89
5.6.1 Flygt (lost LOM)	89
5.6.2 Rapid Tooling for Wax Moulding	90
5.6.3 Case Study from IVF Stockholm	94

6 DIGITISING AND LMT — 95
6.1 REVERSE ENGINEERING — 95
6.2 DIGITISING — 96
6.3 MODEL CREATION — 97
6.4 CASE — 97

7 COMMUNICATION — 99
7.1 FAST COMMUNICATIONS — 99
7.2 ISDN AND VIDEO CONFERENCES — 100
7.3 COLLABORATIVE COMPUTING — 101
7.4 HOW DOES IT WORK? — 102

8. INDUSTRIAL CASE STUDIES — 106
8.1 NEW TECHNOLOGY AND FLOW OF INFORMATION — 106
8.1.1 Design and product development — 106
8.1.2 Prototypes — 109
8.1.3 Industrialisation — 109
8.2 STEP OVERVIEW AND CURRENT STATUS — 111
8.2.1 Summary — 111
8.2.2 Definitions — 111
8.2.3 Scenarios for the Application of STEP — 111
8.2.4 Motivation for a Standard — 112
8.2.5 The Product Model Concept — 113
8.2.6 The STEP Structure — 113
8.2.7 Overview and Fundamental Principles — 114
8.2.8 Description Methods — 114
8.2.9 Implementation Methods — 114
8.2.10 Conformance Testing Methodology and Framework — 115
8.2.11 Generic Resources — 115
8.2.12 Application Resources — 115
8.2.13 Application Protocols — 116
8.2.14 Abstract Test Suites — 117
8.2.15 Conclusion — 117
8.3 LAERDAL AND THE NOR/LMT PROJECT — 118
8.4 CERAMIC CORES CAST IN A CORE BOX — 120
8.4.1 Background — 120
8.4.2 Implementation — 120
8.4.3 Conclusion — 121
8.5 NEW DIGITISING DEVICE AT HUT — 122

8.5.1 Application Example	124
8.6 MATERIAL AND FUNCTION TESTING	124
8.7 WATER JET IMPELLER	126
8.7.1 Tooling of Prototype and Digitising	127
8.7.2 3D-CAD-Modelling	128
8.7.3 Rapid Prototyping	129
8.7.4 Soft Tooling and Investment Casting	129

9 PROCESS PLANNING AND RPT — 131

9.1 RPT VS CONVENTIONAL MANUFACTURING	132
9.2 PROCESS PLANNING FOR INDIVIDUAL RPT PROCESSES	133
9.3 PROCESS PLANNING FOR PROCESS CHAINS	134
9.4 PROCESS PLANNING FOR SELECTING A SUITABLE	135

1 THE PROJECT

1.1 BACKGROUND

One of the important factors making a company competitive is to reduce the product development lead-time. If this time is shorter than that of competitors a company get more orders to better prices. In the free European market this will be more and more important in the years to come.

The length of the lead-time is strongly influenced by two factors. The first is the experimentation and testing necessary to determine a product's shape and dimensions giving the optimal design in relation to function and cost. This could be the shaping of the visual image of a product, ergonomic studies and technical tests, flow tests of cooling channels or model turbines, or just to check if parts actually fit together. A major problem in this area is the lack of a methodology which could be used for a systematic reduction of a product's lead-time in small and medium sized industries in the Nordic countries.

The other factor strongly influencing the product lead-time is the production of a variety of "help objects". This could be the production of models of all kinds, such as models for flow tests of water turbine wheels, models for visual evaluation and functional tests, and casting models. It does also include the production of jigs and fixtures as well as tooling in general. Especially the production of forming tools is often time critical, as it is for instance in batch-production of aluminium profiles. In such a case the actual production of an order typically takes a day or less, while the production and testing of the tools takes 2 months. If we could reduce the tool production time, it would have a dramatic impact on the time of delivery in the company.

The reason why we believe a great impact could be reached in this area now is the know-how we have about the exploding technology called "Layer Manufacturing".

1.2 LAYER MANUFACTURING

Layer Manufacturing (LMT) is one of many names given to the new branch of production technologies, which first was brought into the market in 1988. Today our estimate is that it is around 50 different processes available, being of different stages of development [see NI's book: Layer Manufacturing - A Challenge of the Future].

It started with plastic objects, but now the first metal and ceramics processes are in the market. In the Nordic countries this development has been taken very seriously and industry is heavily engaged. This is the reason why we got such a large involvement in the project.

Today we have a large number of LMT machines in operation in the Nordic countries. This spans many different types of machines using paper, plastics and metal. as part material. Each of these machines cost in order of magnitude 3-4 mill. NOK, and since we in the Nordic countries already have three generation machines starting in 1989, it is clear that the only sensible way in order to stay on the leading edge in this technology is a co-operation between the countries and between the institutes and industry. It is in fact realistic for the time being for small and medium sized industry to buy their own equipment since the development is so fast that they will end up with outdated equipment after a short time. We therefore advocate that industry should co-operate with institutes and together develop how the technology should be utilised in the best possible way. This could be done since the capacity on the existing machines is great enough to cover the industrial need on a short term basis.

We see such a co-operation model to be the best way to handle this exploding technology and still compete with the larger countries in Europe. Some Nordic institutes have expressed their long term goal to be the leading milieus in Europe in the LMT field. This imply they have to invest in new equipment each time a major breakthrough takes place. This is challenging and it has the positive effect that Nordic industry could be kept on the leading edge through co-operative projects covering the enormous changes taking place in production technology today.

1.3 OVERALL GOAL

The project goal was to establish an inter-Nordic network of competence in the LMT-area consisting of:

1.3 OVERALL GOAL

- up to 40 companies being knowledgeable in the LMT-technology, and having practical experience and know-how about how to benefit from its use in their own operation
- centres of competence in which companies can have models, prototypes or parts made to their needs fast and accurate

The project should implement and test out a new methodology in product and process design based on an intensive use of models at an early stage in the design process. The project should further implement and test the use of LMT-models on a broad base in the Nordic casting industry. Finally, the project will establish a high velocity ISDN-network between companies and LMT-centres participating in the various stages of the product development process, and to perform an efficient transfer of know-how to industry via newsletters, conferences and by writing a book.

1.4 PARTNERS

In the planning stage the project has altogether 40 partners. Since then some have come and some have gone. In the final stage the following 32 companies and institutions were partners:

Denmark:
- Coloplast A/S
- Danfoss A/S
- Dansk Teknologisk Institut
- Lego Engineering A/S
- Lego Futura ApS
- LK A/S
- W. Svanemose A/S

Finland
- FF-Jet Ltd. Ab
- HUT
- Kemira Safety Oy
- Neopoli Oy
- Planmeca Oy
- SacoTec Oy
- TP-Kunnossapito Oy

Norway
- EPM Consultants AS
- Industriell Produktservice AS
- Kværner Eureka AS
- Jac Jacobsen AS
- Laerdal
- NTNU-SINTEF

Sweden
- Ermator AB
- Essge-Plast AB
- Hackås Precisionsgjuteri AB
- Husqvarna AB, Trandsbyfabriken
- IIT Flygt AB
- IVF
- Jonsson & Paulsson Industri AB
- KOINOR AB
- Liljefors & Rosell
- SIGMA Design & Development AB
- TPC Trustor Precision Components
- Volvo Aero Corporation

These 31 partners represents companies, consulting companies, institutes, and universities.

The project board has consisted of the following persons:
- Øyvind Bjørke, NTNU-SINTEF, Norway
- Bent Mieritz, DTI, Denmark
- Berndt Øquist, KOINOR AB, Sweden
- Jukka Tuomi, HUT, Finland
- Berndt Holmer, IVF, Sweden
- Urban Harryson, IVF, Sweden

The project co-ordinator has been: Øyvind Bjørke, NTNU-SINTEF

1.5 WORK PROGRAM

The work program consists of 6 work packages, and they are described in the following:

1.5.1 Work package 1: Design methodology with intensive use of models

Layer Manufacturing used in connection with product and process development will secure a faster, better and cheaper development which in turn will result in a greater potential for profit by an increased sale. Using LMT will influence the traditional way of product development methods. The habits must change according to a new philosophy incorporated when new technology is available. The important phrases in this connection are:

- *Changes and corrections only in the very beginning*
- *Use the majority of efforts early in the development phase*
- *From sequential to parallel product development*
- *Measure the critical paths and bottlenecks only*
- *Use CAD/CAE/RPT technologies*
- *Human co-operation and communication*

Task 1.1 Registration of present working procedures and resource consumption in product and process development, considered generally and elucidate the starting point. All parties involved should have a mutual understanding of the present situation so the results can be estimated and measured more easily as a termination of the project. Developing a start seminar for managers, project leaders and R&D employees, where attitudes are influenced and plans are made in accordance with the aim of the project.
Detailed planning in the individual companies of the actual projects and how and when to use, design models, functional models, models for sales and marketing, and models for production improvement and prototypes.
The use of 3D CAD on your own or other equipment is analysed and chosen. The application of other auxiliary tools such as calculation and simulation when geometry of the object has been decided in 3D CAD.

Task 1.2 Implementation of the seminars in the individual companies and in groups of companies. Methodology and working procedures from design via construction and process development to a finished product are implemented. Structure of the decision for the most expedient procedure is estimated, chosen and proved in the actual development of the companies.

Methodology or "models of a parallel learning system" and models for "ideal organisation" for maximum reduction of development time will be developed.

The use of 2D and 3D CAD is described and the results of the LMT process/models are estimated.

The development tasks are completed and state-of-the-art in each company is described. The evaluation should especially describe the ideal "organising model" for maximum reduction of development by using LMT. This must be described by means of methodology, organisation, information flow (human and data) and communication.

1.5.2 Work package 2: Use of Layer Manufacturing in Casting

Layer manufacturing used in connection with all types of casting processes is probably the most promising application area for LMT. By it's nature LMT is a technique for bringing complex shaped models quick from design to reality. In all the different casting processes in use they always make a master model, either for a prototype casting in a low series production, in order to prepare the final production, or directly in the production casting, as done with traditional sand casting.

Casting covers several different processes, from the traditional sand casting to high precision investment casting of high precision parts. The list below shows the different casting techniques to be covered in the project:

- *Sand casting*
- *Die casting*
- *Investment casting*
- *Plaster casting*
- *Rubber plaster casting*
- *Silicon mould*

Task 2.1 **Sand casting.** Produce a complete set of patterns and core boxes based on layer manufacturing prepared and tailored for prototype casting.

Task 2.2 **Plaster and rubber casting.** Produce and prepare all the necessary masters and cores bases on layer manufacturing and advanced 3D CAD for making high precision castings both in plaster and rubber plaster

1.5 WORK PROGRAM 7

processes. A comparison of the results with traditional methods is a key element.

Task 2.3 **Lost wax and lost plastics casting.** By filling a cavity with wax it is possible to make a lost wax casting by dipping the wax master in a ceramic slurry, burn out the wax and pour metal into the shell. The cavity will be made as an LMT object. An evaluation and test of cost benefits of LMT moulds relative NC machined moulds is a key activity.

Task 2.4 **Injection mould.** Production of cavities for prototype injection moulds for plastics based on the use of LMT models directly.

1.5.3 Work package 3: 3D digitising and LMT in combination

The combination of 3D digitising and LMT holds the promise of further possibilities for reduction of product development lead-time. One example is through a pragmatic and test oriented procedure where one:

- perform tests on a prototype made by LMT
- modify it directly through machining or manual shaping
- then digitises it in order to update the CAD model
- in order to make a new prototype by LMT.

Especially when aesthetic or ergonomic aspects are important manual shaping is a natural way of making at least a part of the work which makes subsequent 3D digitising and LMT verification/model-making very attractive. "Reversed engineering" measuring existing products in order to have a base for modification, further development or tool making, although used today, could be used much more by companies of all sizes.

So far digitising has been a slow process as both the actual measurements and the creating of the actual CAD model form the digitised data are time consuming. Though much work remains to be done on the software side in particular, this technology, stimulated not least by the LMT development, is moving quickly with laser scanning, photogrammetric and other methods adding to the traditional co-ordinate measuring machines.

Here it is suggested to promote the combined use of 3D digitising and LMT as tools for potentially great importance for, among others, companies engaged in industrial design and tool making.

Task 3.1 Summarise user needs and compile profiles for digitising and LMT methods. Choose test cases and carry out in an interactive manner digitising, CAD modelling and LMT modelling. Generalise the results, describe methods to get around limitations and make efficient use of 3D digitising and LMT as they exist.

1.5.4 Work package 4: A feasibility study of computer-aided process planning for LMT processes

Planning an LMT run consists, among other things, of analysing the model and choosing a suitable orientation of the part. In the case of the design a choice between different LMT processes to be made and this decision is based on several factors. One of these is the accuracy of the process: Can the process reproduce all the features in this model well enough? For complex shapes this can be a difficult task. Software tools that could analyse a model and to identify possible problems areas and/or help the machine operator to prepare a run could be named *process planning tools for LMT processes*.

Task 4.1 A feasibility study of the problems and possibilities by making a process planning system for LMT processes should be undertaken. If a positive result is obtained a plan for the development of such a system should be set up.

1.5.5 Work package 5: Establish ISDN networks between companies and LMT centres

Increased application of 3D CAD and LMT technology in industry means increased demands on the ability of transmit this information between the companies and R&D organisations participating in the various stages of the product development process. In a short perspective it is particularly important that companies with 3D CAD constructions, who do not have LMT equipment themselves for producing models and prototypes, can use high velocity network for transmission of digital information between companies, LMT centres, and specialists such as foundries and tool makers who they are dependent on.

Task 5.1 Effort will be spent into organising and establishing a functional ISDN network between the participating companies and the Scandinavian LMT centres. This ISDN network will ensure a fast and safe transmission of text, sound and images as well as enabling a quick and cost-effective transmission of a large quantity of data between the companies, LMT centres and specialists. The ISDN network will also be used to quickly and effectively carry out knowledge and necessary discussions with the participating companies. If possible this will be done via picture-phones or videos, thus saving time and cutting out

1.5 WORK PROGRAM

misunderstanding and doubts at an early stage of the product development process.

1.5.6 Work package 6: Technology transfer and networks for LMT

Increased knowledge and proficiency concerning the use of LMT within Nordic industries will be achieved by allowing both large, but especially small companies to practically try out LMT in different stages of the product development process.

Different technology transfer activities will be performed spreading knowledge and proficiency of the LMT technology within Nordic industries thus enabling them better judgement of where, in a product development process, LMT has its strongest points and even restrictions, and when it is technically and economically practical to use LMT in a product development process.

Task 6.1 Seminars and theme days will be arranged where the participants can learn of the results achieved within the different areas of application and use of the "tools" and methods produced to make easier the appeasement of the technology and when it best should be introduced into the company.

Task 6.2 Newsletters will by the quarter be given out thus enabling a greater spreading of the results which have gradually been achieved during a project period.

Task 6.3 A Competence Network consisting of LMT centres and companies using different casting processes will be organised. The competence network will also be given an important role in the technology transfer activities and in giving advises when LMT should be most effectively used. The ISDN network will also be used in these activities.

2. SUMMARY OF RESULTS

2.1 LMT MACHINES IN THE NORDIC COUNTRIES

It is today 27 LMT machines scattered around in the Nordic countries. Many of these have been involved in the NOR-LMT project. In the following a summary of the existing LMT machines are given and their location are drawn in the map.

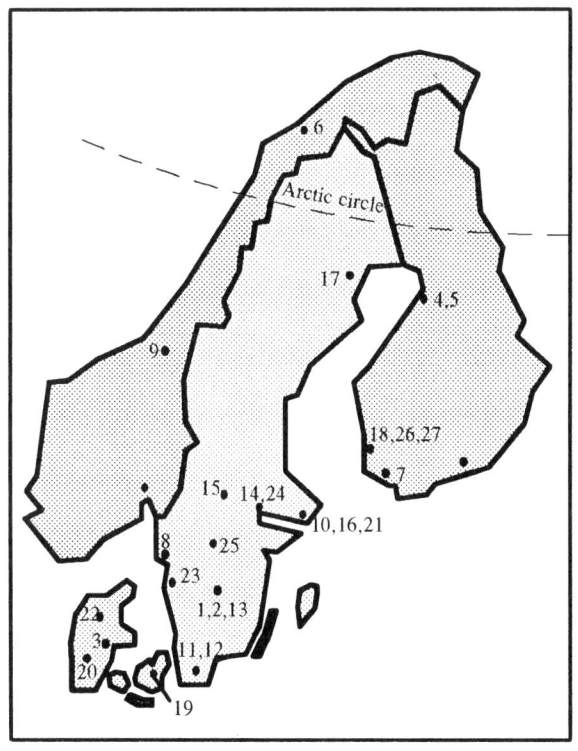

Figure 2.1. Map of the Location of LMT Machines in the Nordic Countries.

Ref	Vend./proc.	Model	User	Cont.person	Phone/fax
1	3D Systems	SLA 250	Electrolux Rapid	Svenssen	+46 36 14 63 58
2	SLA	SLA 500	Dev. Huskvarna, S		+46 36 14 67 10 fax
3	3D Systems	SLA 250	DTI Produktutvikl.	Wonsild	+45 89 43 84 01
	SLA		Aarhus, DK		+45 89 43 84 25 fax
4	3D Systems	SLA 250	Oulu Inst. of Tech.	Alamäki	+358 81 5370 411
5	SLA		Oulu, SF		+358 81 5370 400 fax
6	3D Systems	SLA 250	HIN/VINN	Koch	+47 76 92 21 84
	SLA		Narvik, N		+47 76 94 48 66 fax
7	3D Systems	SLA 250	Nokia NMP Oy,	Syrjälä	+358 10 5052 590
	SLA		Salo, SF		+358 10 5052 999 fax
8	3D Systems	SLA 500	Caran Total Design	Landström	+46 522 393 20
	SLA		Uddevalla, S		+46 522 339 51 fax
9	Cubital	Solider	SINTEF Pro.Teknik	Ruud	+47 73 59 71 25
	SGC	5600	Trondheim, N		+47 73 59 36 70 fax
10	DTM	Sinterst.	IVF-KTH	Killander	+46 8 21 98 64
	SLS	200	Stockholm, S		+46 8 20 22 27 fax
11	Stratasys	FDM-1600	Verkstedtekniskt	Tufvesson	+46 411 747 32
12	FDM	2 st	centrum,Ystad, S		+46 411 156 22 fax
13	Stratasys	FDM-1600	WIBA AB	Wiking	+46 36 13 37 00
	FDM		Huskvarna, S		+46 36 14 30 38 fax
14	Stratasys	FDM-1600	Modellteknik AB	Andersson	+46 16 11 45 70
	FDM		Eskilstuna, S		+46 16 12 07 40 fax
15	Stratasys	FDM-1600	CREATOR	Thordmark	+46 225 351 00
	FDM		Vikmanshyttan, S		+46 225 307 93 fax
16	Stratasys	FDM-1600	Emanon	Skogh	+46 8 624 25 10
	FDM		Stocksund, S		+46 8 624 25 12 fax
17	Stratasys	FDM-1600	Caran Prod. Dev.	Stenlund	+46 911 766 00
	FDM		Piteå, S		+46 911 766 09 fax
18	Stratasys	FDM-1600	Turku Inst.Techn.	Seppänen	+358 21 3370 698
	FDM		Turku, SF		+358 21 3370 791 fax
19	Stratasys	FDM-1600	Damvig	Damvig	+45 43 993 736
	FDM		Taastrup, DK		
20	Stratasys	FDM-1600	Lego Engineering	Behnke	+45 753 311 88
	FDM		Billund, DK		
21	Stratasys	FDM-1600	ProTECH AB	Ottoson	+46 8 62 00 48
	FDM		Sollentuna, S		+46 8 92 96 20 fax
22	Stratasys	FDM-1600	Ide-Pro	Nors	+45 975 248 38
	FDM		Skive, DK		+45 975 265 26 fax
23	Helisys	LOM-2030	IVF	Harrysson	+46 31 706 60 85
	LOM		Gøteborg, S		+46 31 27 61 30 fax
24	Helisys	LOM-2030	Eskilst. Modellsn.	Carlsson	+46 16 51 88 88
	LOM		Eskilstuna, S		+46 16 51 60 54 fax
25	Helisys	LOM-2030	Plastic Des.& Serv.	Thorstenson	+46 510 506 11
	LOM		Vinninga, S		+46 510 506 27 fax
26	EOS	M	Electrolux Rapid	Syrjälä	+358 21 4399600
27	EOSint	M 250	Develop.Rusko, SF		+358 21 4399620 fax

2.1 LMT MACHINES IN THE NORDIC COUNTRIES

The above table shows the types of machines, the owner, the contact person in the organisations, and the phone and fax numbers.

2.2 GENERAL BENEFITS

2.2.1 Application Areas

Applications in the area of creative design are many. This spans from the use as a mean to find design errors till the use in the marketing process. The prime application covered in the project was design methodology.

An important concept in this context is *"Rapid Product Development"*. This expression reflects the idea that product development concepts like *Rapid Prototyping* and *Reverse Engineering,* and methods like *Concurrent Engineering, Quality Function Deployment* and others, can be considered as supplementary tools aiming at better and cheaper products brought into market with a shorter lead time.

A major portion of the project has been devoted towards applications in casting. LMT is a method for production of one or few of a kind. It is therefore specially applicable for production of casting patterns and tooling.

There are several ways of using LMT as a tool for making castings, but the three main principles are:

1. Casting patterns directly made by the LMT method. According to this principle a model is made for each casting. The procedure is mostly used for lost wax casting.
2. Casting moulds directly made by the LMT method. According to this principle the negative geometry is made of the part that is to be manufactured. This is contrary to the first principle. Also for this principle there is one mould for each casting.
3. Patterns and moulds indirectly made by the LMT method. According to this principle the tools to be used in the foundry process are made by the LMT method. Thus it is possible to make several articles at a time. Some examples are patterns and core boxes for sand casting, tools to make wax patterns for the lost wax process, tools for plaster casting or core boxes for die casting.

LMT models are also capable of direct production of tools for investment casting for making prototype series of plastic parts.

Another area of applications is reverse engineering. Reverse engineering is a general description of a process where the aim is the creation of a computer model by measuring an already existing physical model. The computer model will then be used for manufacturing of new physical models, maybe in other materials and maybe after the computer model has been modified. It may also be used for manufacturing a tool for making the physical parts.

Finally, fast communication is a necessity in future product development. Increased application of 3D CAD and LMT technology in industry means increased demands on the ability to transmit this information between the companies and R&D-organisations participating in the different stages of the product development process. In a short term perspective it is particularly important that the companies with 3D CAD-designs, which do not have LMT-equipment themselves for producing models and prototypes, can use high velocity network for transmission of digital information between companies, LMT-centres and specialists such as foundries and toolmakers on whom they are dependent.

Efforts were spent in organising and establishing a functional ISDN-network between the participating Nordic LMT-centres at the very start of the project. This ISDN-network was planned to ensure a fast and safe transmission of test, sound, images as well as enabling a quick and cost-effective transmission of a large quantity of data between LMT-centres, specialists and companies

2.2.2 Increased Know-how

The project has resulted in increased know-how in the 32 companies taking part in the project. They have got experiences in both the strong and weak aspects of LMT processes. This has brought them in position better to judge when it is time to change the existing technology. The focus has further been brought to the urgent need for 3D-CAD systems. Within the new area, 3D-CAD systems have been a precondition for further progress.

Also in the institutes the project has resulted in increased know-how in the LMT area. The institutes will also after the project ends proceed to perform a continuos technology transfer to industry. Another important effect is that the institutes via the co-operating universities will get the know-how out to the students, bringing the futures engineers to a higher level of knowledge in the LMT area. The book may be used as course material in this educational process.

2.3 MAJOR RESULTS

2.3.1 Design Methodology

It has been developed a new design methodology, based on an intensive use of CAD/CAE/LMT and high speed communication, as the vehicle to reach the new goals in the design process. Such objectives are to reduce changes in a late stage in

2.3 MAJOR RESULTS

a development project and to move from a sequential to a parallel product development process. Further to put effort on the critical path and the bottlenecks in the process. Finally to put priority on human co-operation and communication.

2.3.2 LMT in Casting

A majority of work has been put into the use of LMT in order to improve casting. This is the area in which most progress took place in the project period. Specially, a broad development took place in: Sand casting, die casting, investment casting, plaster casting, rubber casting, and silicon mould casting. The use in industry of these methods has increased dramatically as a result of the development. Specially, the car industry and the pump- and turbine industries has really taken off in a systematically use of LMT. This is shown among others by the increased number of projects run by the LMT oriented institutes which are demonstrated by the examples shown in this book, and off the large number of developments project which have taken place in the period, but which could not be reported due to the confidential character of the projects.

2.3.3 3D Digitising and LMT in Combination

Reversed engineering is also an area in growth. This because a design often starts from an existing product. By a digitising of the existing model, a 3D geometric model of the product may be set up. Based on this new geometric model a LMT model may be produced. This is a fruitful way to go in many industrial cases. The procedure has been tested out during the project with good results.

2.3.4 Computer Aided Process Planning for LMT Processes

A feasibility study of a process planning system has been performed in the project. This has led to specifications for a future development.

2.3.5 High Speed Communication

The project has tested out the use of ISDN networks in the communication process between product developers, foundries, producers, and LMT centres. The cheap and fast transfer of large data volumes such as geometrical models and STL-files for production of prototypes, has shown a great progress. The exchange and "repair" of data files are brought into professionalism. Further, the on-line discussion between the different partners in the product development process has grown out of its childhood and has become real life practice among companies and institutes.

2.3.6 Technology Transfer

A. very important part of the project has been the dissemination of the developed information. This has been performed through a numerous of national and international meetings. It has also been done by giving out a newsletter within the project, quarterly. This has kept the partners, and the large part of industry to which it has been distributed, up to date with the developments in the project, but also of the international trends. Further, the project has arranged conferences in the Nordic countries annually, by which the results have been published and discussed. Finally, the writing and publishing of this book represents the final contribution to the technology transfer performed by the NOR-LMT project.

3 PROGRESS IN THE FIELD OF LMT

Since 1992 the RP-industry has experienced accelerating expansion. Each year the total number of machines sold annually has increased by approximately one hundred units. New techniques have entered the market at the average rate of one per year. The growth in the number both of different available systems and purchased units has stimulated the supply of related accessories, software and services. By December 1994 the total amount of systems sold to date was some 900 units and during the same year RP-market revenue grew 100 % reaching almost 200 million US$. The 1995 market was expected to exceed 318 million US$ [1,2].

Although one might expect the opposite, the co-existence of rival techniques has not reduced the system purchasing prices significantly. New manufacturers have gained their market share from the growth and major price competition is yet to come. Some manufacturers have even raised their prices due to the availability of new, technically improved models. Though some lately introduced new machines do break this pattern, it is still too early to say whether they can be seen as a sign of the beginning of an era of cheaper RP-units or as an indication of the generally expected split in the RP-market [3].

Most of the RP manufacturers and experts predict that in the near future rapid prototyping units will be divided into two categories. The first one consists of cheap and simple machines capable of operating in an office environment. They are intented mainly for visualising and making mock-ups and therefore their accuracy and the material strength of the parts produced need not fulfil actual production line demands. The other category includes 'traditional' RP-units, which are designed to perform with the best possible accuracy, speed and part material strength. Price is therefore more or less a secondary criterion in their design. These machines will be used to produce testable prototypes, test series and actual mass production tools. While the first category of units are to be used in offices, the second type are to be located at plant floors of service bureaus and big manufacturers [3].

In any case the demand for cheaper equipment is strong. According to Rapid Prototyping Report's customer inquiry, 40% of its readers find price to be the most important barrier to rapid prototyping's commercial success. So far the response to the demand for cheaper units seems to be inadequate because the price of machines capable of producing high precision and wear resistant parts in adequate time still remains high. Nevertheless the new generation of cheap 'office compatible' machines is a step towards the removal of the major obstacle hindering rapid prototyping from becoming a natural extension of computer based design [1,4,5].

Research in the field is concentrating on mastering the existing systems and finding new methods to improve material strength. In practice this means efforts to make composite, metal and ceramic parts with either existing or brand new techniques. Although there has been some significant progress, the real breakthrough is still a way ahead. The direction of research supports the theory of a dual RP-market because improved part quality automatically changes the role of service bureau from being an expedient medium of design to one closer to the actual production units.

From the software developer's point of view the market has now become large enough to sustain the existence of independent software houses. In addition to this CAD-suppliers have noticed that rapid prototyping is becoming an interesting branch of the design oriented software market. With increased competition the growth of interest has led to more user-friendly interfaces and conversion software becoming available. In the second half of the project period, the design community received the new international CAD-standard STEP and lively discussion continued in the RP-field about the successor to STL-protocol. For the latter several contour-based solutions have been proposed [4].

3.1 PUBLISHED NEW PROCESSES

During the project period two new manufacturers, Sanders Prototype Inc. and BPM Technologies Inc., introduced their solutions for rapid prototyping. The machines are both based on the deposition of molten droplets of thermoplastic material, although the technical implementations are different. These units are already commercially viable. In addition 3D Systems, the largest RP-manufacturer, released the first information on its first non-stereolithography system Multi-Jet Modelling Process (MJM).

3.1 PUBLISHED NEW PROCESSES

3.1.1 Sanders Prototype Inc.

Despite the fact that precision deposition of molten droplets is one of the oldest ideas for additive fabrication, it took until spring 1994 before the first commercial unit based on the idea was introduced [6]. Sanders Prototype Inc. describes the process as 3D Plotting and the latest model in the Model Maker series is denoted MM-6PRO. Sanders developed the technology in partnership with the arms and defence enterprise E-Systems, the role of which has now diminished to hold only 10 % of the company's shares. The following technical description is based mainly on information provided by the company.

The machine is rather small, (445 mm x 521 mm x 584 mm [wlh]) without display and keyboard. Besides a normal household mains supply no other connections or ventilation are needed. The heart of the system is a liquid-to-solid inkjet plotter with separate jets for build and support material. In order to build a model in successive layers the print head moves in X-Y -plane and build surface in Z-direction. The X-Y drive carriage also holds a flatbed milling subsystem to machine the layer smooth at the end of the build cycle. Thus the system can maintain precise information about the model's current height and prevent possible deviations in previous layers from being multiplied.

The milling unit can also be used to repair defected layers. Among several other operational conditions the correct function of the jets is automatically monitored. In case of malfunction the nozzles are cleaned, the layers built since the previous check are milled away and the build process is continued from that point. These features allow for independent operation between material refilling and normal maintenance routines. Depending on the geometry of the part and the fill pattern which is used, the material supplies may even last as long as 12 hours. It is possible to halt the process temporarily for part or machine overhaul without loss of accuracy.

At the beginning of each build cycle, the layer and cavity outlines are drawn with one or more adjacent walls depending on the required surface finish. To optimise material consumption and delivery time the model can be built in three ways: hollow, with a cellular fill pattern, or as a solid part. Support material is deposited according to a pre-determined model under overhangs and cavities.

In MM-6PRO the layer thickness can be adjusted between 12.7 µm and 76.2 µm. In order to simplify the user interface, the company software provides six standard grades because non standard layer thickness adjustment requires a setting of over 100 parameters. At the moment the software lets the operator use two different layer thickness in a single part, but the automatic selection of slice thickness will be available in the near future [7]. The accuracy of the Z-axis positioning is 3.2 µm.

The droplet diameter is 76.2 µm and the droplet positioning accuracy in X-Y-directions is 6.4 µm resulting in a wall thickness of 101.6 µm. The company representative says that in their own experiments, by using special techniques, they have managed to make such features as a box with a wall thickness and an opening of 50.8 μm[7]. The company promises 50 μm dimensional tolerance over the machine's (152 mm × 152 mm × 152 mm) build volume. Surface roughness is said to be 1.5 - 2.5 μm depending on the source.

The build material ProtoBuild has similar characteristics to common investment casting waxes except that it has over two times the mechanical strength. The support material ProtoSupport is a blend of natural and synthetic waxes and fatty esters. ProtoBuild melts at 94 - 106°C and ProtoSupport at 54 - 76°C. For dewaxing the company recommends BIOACTC VSO in which ProtoSupport is soluble. To ease cleaning, the build material is dyed green and the support material red. Both support and build materials are non-toxic. BIOACT has low order toxicity and flash point in 102°C. No other materials are available at the moment [7].

The standard interface is a program called TMM which allows the user to observe the model as a whole or in individual slices, make simple corrections, create support structures, set the process parameters and monitor the process itself. The program can convert STL-, pre-sliced HPGL- and several other CAD-files to the Model Maker System binary file format. In addition to the company's own supply there are some third party software vendors [9,10].

Due to its size, clean and automated operation and available operator friendly programs MM-6BPRO is well-suited to the office environment. Only the task of cleaning the parts is a messy, time and labour demanding process. When a part is ready the support wax is washed away with a solvent either manually or in a special cleaning device. The company claims that no part swelling occurs during the cleaning. The system costs approximately 60 000 US$ [3,11].

3.1.2 BPM Technologies Inc.

The founder of the company, William E. Masters was awarded the first patent concerning precision droplet stream manufacturing. The patent application for a method called 'Ballistic Particle Manufacturing' (also the origin of the acronym in the company's name) was filed in 1984 and the patent issued in 1987. It describes the principles of a system that creates the desired shape by shooting molten plastic or metal droplets accurately to the substrate. Each droplet can be directed individually which allows tangential depositing of part walls thus enabling construction of hollow and overhanging structures without support arrangements. The company calls this arrangement continuous articulation to surface normals, CAN, also known as Various Desktop Jetting Systems.

The free orientation of the jetting direction places high demands on both the controlling program and the mechanism itself. Mathematically, the system forms a

3.1 PUBLISHED NEW PROCESSES

6- or 7-dimensional space (x, y, z, φ, θ, t + one extra dimension if the print head's rotation around its own longitudinal axis has to be taken into account). In this space the controlling system must prevent collisions between the print head, manipulators and model. Because the system does not use supporting wax or any other corresponding means the droplet stream must always be aimed towards the solid substrate. When making horizontal overhangs or cantilevers the jetting direction must also be horizontal or near it. Thus the program has to convert the original file to suitable print head positions and movements whilst simultaneously keeping track of the completed parts of the model. The difficulties mentioned above and problems with the droplet ejecting system may explain why the company's commercial launch of the product was delayed until spring 1995. However, the result is the first rapid prototyping unit which does not rely strictly on manufacturing in layers [6,8].

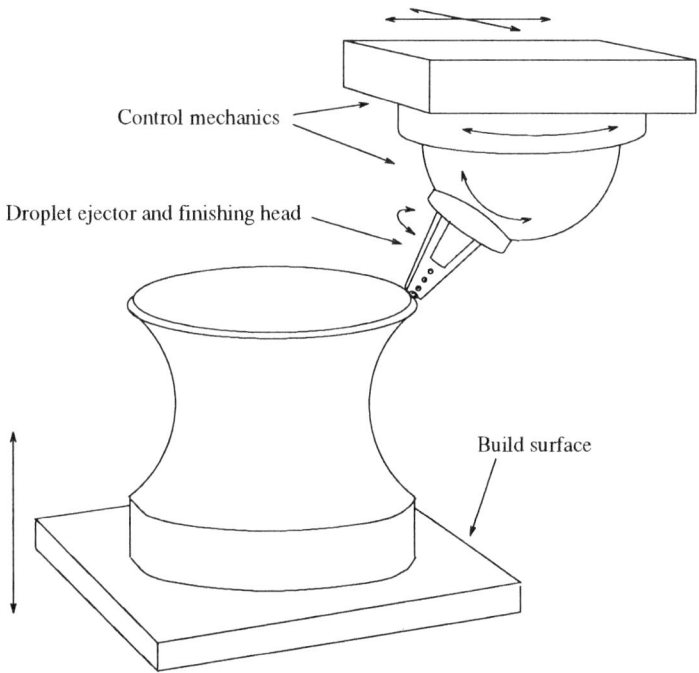

Figure 3.1. Schematic Representation of 3D Object Printer's Build Unit.

Personal Modeler as the company calls their only commercial model so far, is the cheapest RP-unit available at the moment. The price is between 29 000 and 35 000 US$, depending on optional equipment. The basic model consists of a build unit and control computer with a tilt-out colour display and keyboard integrated in a tower-like unit (size 610 mm × 500 mm × 1370 mm). It weighs 68 kg and is mounted on wheels for ease of movement. The machine runs on the network current and its clean operation means that it does not require any air conditioning or cooling arrangements. The standard software can utilise STL -files which are fed in on 3.5" floppy disks. More versatile software, internal modem and Ethernet card are available as accessories.

In action the ceramic ejector controlled by a piezoelectric oscillator shoots 12 000 droplets per second. The 75 µm diameter droplets solidify and flatten to 50 µm when hitting the substrate surface. Before the droplets are fully hardened the ejector head is followed by another heated head that smoothens the surface resulting in approximately 6 µm surface roughness.

One can measure the result with stereolithography units which are regarded as the most accurate on the market at present. For example 3D Systems claim that their machines can attain 3 µm roughness on vertical surfaces and 0.2 µm on flat horizontal surfaces. In comparison one must remember that due to the tangential direction no stair stepping exists in BPM's system and therefore part fidelity may have to be judged on a somewhat different basis.

According to some reports there have been problems with reliability and part quality. Also the speed of the single jet process has been questioned. The company claims that the machine can build most of the parts "overnight", and has announced that they are working on software improvements in order to "achieve a significant increase in speed". Current technology allows for a tripling of the deposition rate which would mean a 250 % increase in the build rate. Further speed improvements can be gained with multiple head configurations. The multi-jet approach would also allow coloured models - and increase software complexity exponentially [13,14].

Despite having the ability to deposit horizontally, the 3D Object Printer does have to use support structures in the case of long, self-supporting cantilevers and overhangs. In these cases the accessory software has basic routines for repairing STL-files and the automatic creation of supports. It can define the part's position in the build envelope so that the minimal amount of supports is needed. The supports are made of the same material as the part itself, but the machine automatically creates perforation at junctions to minimise the cleanup and finishing work. No other post-processing actions are required

Models are built hollow in order to achieve minimum delivery time and material cost. When additional strength is needed a cellular fill pattern can be used. Because material is neither milled away nor wasted in any other way and because supports are minimal, the material consumption is kept down. The company claims that the average material cost per part is US$1. the largest possible part size is (250 mm x 203 mm x 150 mm) For the time being the only available material is a non-toxic thermoplastic that resembles investment casting waxes. It melts at temperatures of 105 to 110°C, its specific gravity is 0.9 and price about 165 US$/kg. The colour of the material is white but the manufacturer can supply different dyed options if there is enough demand [8,15,16].

3.2 MATERIAL DEVELOPMENT

Material research has been lively during the past two years. Beside the search for wear resistance the selection of other features - like RP-rubbers - was also extended. This chapter lists and briefly describes the most significant improvements made commercial in the course of the project. Because of the activity in the field and somewhat restricted scope of this book, only the real milestones have gained attention here at the expense of more minor achievements.

Significant safety improvements were achieved with less-toxic or non-toxic resins for SLS- and SGC-systems. First direct RP-metal process was developed by the joint efforts of EOS GmbH, Germany and Electrolux Rapid Development, Finland. Other interesting novelties included a plastic material for LOM and DTM glass-filled nylon and binder coated steel powders for SLS.

3.2.1 Metals

For the time being, only selective laser sintering has proved to be suitable for making metallic parts. However, the mechanism of sintering incorporates some problems that need to be overcome before the result fulfils the requirements of rapid prototyping.

When a powder is sintered below melting point the driving force of the process is the tendency to minimise the free energy by minimising the surface. The particles fuse together and the material diffuses to junction areas so that empty spaces between the particles diminish and packing density increases. The more dense the part becomes the more it shrinks and this may cause serious deviations from the original shape. With metals oxidation has to be taken into account as well.

When using metals the laser power becomes crucial. In addition to cost, the increased laser power increases the smallest possible focal diameter i.e. the theoretical resolution of the equipment decreases. Although the required laser power would be available the interaction time between the beam and individual particles remains short because of the spot size and practical manufacturing time. This interaction time may be too short to complete the diffusion process especially for metals with high melting-points.

On the other hand, if there is too much power the powder melts and due to the surface tension, forms a drop the of same size as the spot diameter, the resulting part is very porous and de-laminated. The laser power required can be reduced either by pre-heating or by increasing the work chamber pressure, both of which are technically complex and expensive solutions. Another possibility is to use a mixture or an alloy of high- and low-melting metals when the latter melts and fuses the particles together. If wetting occurs the molten phase also creates capillary pressure between the solid particles and thus promotes sintering within the limitations of interaction time. The dual phase approach does not inhibit shrinking [17,18,19].

EOSINT-M Electrolux Rapid Development in Rusko, Finland, has developed and patented the first real RP-metal which allows the manufacturing of metallic parts directly, without pre- or post-processing. It is marketed by Electro Optical Systems GmbH (EOS) to be used in their EOSINT-M -series selective laser sintering machines. The process does not require pre-heating or shield gas and the material does not shrink during sintering. The strength and machinability of the material corresponds to that of aluminium but the material itself is porous. The strength can be improved by infiltrating the parts with metal of a low melting temperature or epoxy resin.

The dimensional stability of the material is achieved by combining the physical properties of three different powder components (here A, B and C). The exact physical process is still not clear but the following description gives the presumed outlines of the reaction as described in the patent. Component C shrinks normally during sintering and principally defines the part's strength and surface finish. Components A and B form the expanding part of the mixture compensating the shrinkage of part C. To make this possible, component A must have a higher melting point than the other two components and all the components must be soluble with each other.

At the sintering temperature melting B- and non-melting A-constituent begin to dissolve into each other. However, due to the curvature effect, the smaller particles have higher free energy and thus a greater tendency to form solutions. If the non-melting part consists of relatively large particles, the diffusion from the molten phase to the solid phase is faster than vice versa and the particles grow. The resulting solid solution of A and B has a greater volume than the original volumes of A and B together.

Material characteristics, like the surface finish, can be varied by changing the particle size of component C. The amounts, ratios and particle sizes of A and B have to be adapted to component C, since the particle size affects the dimensional change during sintering. As the reader may have already noticed, suitable choice of A and B components would make the material swell during the process. Final density is about 60 % of the theoretical value.

In the mixture tested by Electrolux the component A is nickel, B includes copper and phosphorus (Cu_3P) and C is a copper based alloy such as brass or bronze. The particle size of A ranges from 100 to 150 µm and the average particle size from 100 to 150 µm. The average particle diameter of component B is less than 50 µm, whereas the particle size of constituent C varies between 5 and 200 µm. Component percentages in weight are approximately 20 - 30 % for A, 5 - 10 % for B and 60 - 75 for C. Sintering temperature is approximately 850°C [20].

3.2 MATERIAL DEVELOPMENT

The material (also called Elux Powder) went through a year's field testing and is now being used by a group of customers, including several service bureau. The main application has been the production of prototype injection moulds. In this use the only required post-processing operation is the surface finishing of the mould in order to remove open surface porosity. Infiltration is required only in production of very large or complex parts when high injection pressure is required.

Electrolux Rapid Development uses the system to provide prototype plastic parts to their customers. The company spokesperson claims that they can send first injection moulded parts to the customer within one working week from when they receive finished CAD- or STL-files. The resulting part surface is matt and smooth, resembling a sand-blasted surface. Further enhancements in surface quality require extra finishing work [21].

During the time the system has been in use no mould breakdown has occurred though prototype series lengths have ranged from 100 to 2000 parts depending on part complexity and the customer's needs. The developers of the powder hint that the mould lifetime may expand drastically if suitable infiltration material is found [22].

EOS policy is to sell machines suited for a specific material such as plastic, metal or sand. The model series are denoted EOSINT-P, -M and -S respectively. The M-series consists of two machines, a laboratory model EOSINT-M160 and a production model M250. The model number denotes, in millimetres, the length of the edge of the cube-shaped build chamber. M160 costs 330 000 US, M250 520 000 US and the powder 215 US/kg [23,24].

DTI Rapid Tool For making metallic parts, that is mainly prototype injection moulds, DTI Corporation has introduced a double phase powder. It consists of low carbon steel particles coated with a polymer binder. The powder is used as normal SLY-materials in a specially equipped Sinterstation 2000. No pre-heating is needed because the power of the laser is sufficient to melt the coating and fuse the particles together.

After the building process the 'green' part is strong enough to withstand being cleaned of excess powder and moved to the furnace where the binder is burned away and the remaining steel particles are sintered together. To minimise shrinkage the part is heated only as much as is required to keep it in one piece. Next the very porous steel part is infiltrated with copper. In a completed part the ratio of steel and copper is approximately 60/40, resulting in physical properties similar to 7075 aluminium, a common prototype tooling material. As the company points out, the process is not capable of producing metallic parts directly and after infiltration the parts require a considerable amount of finishing work.

Despite the precautions the total shrinkage during the process is about two percent. Nevertheless, DTM says that Rapid Tool is dimensionally one of the most accurate of their SLS materials. The company promises that the parts will be accurate to within ± 25 μm for the first two and half centimetres and ± 50 μm for each additional centimetre. The system can deliver the unfinished mould within five days. Another week is required for finishing before the mould can be used in injection moulding.

A Rapid Tool module for an existing Sinterstation 2000 costs 20 000 US$ and a new unit with the module 330 000 US$. Process ovens which, according to the company, have been optimised to speed the binder burn-out and copper infiltration cycle are available at the price of 50 000 US$. The system purchasing price is thus lower than for EOSINT-M but according to the process descriptions EOSINT-M seems to provide shorter time-to-market cycle [13,25,26].

3.2.2 Other new RP-materials

EOSINT-S Another example of innovative thinking in EOS GmbH is their EOSINT-S system. This is a SLS-process designed for the production of sand-casting moulds. The machine uses a resin-coated sand similar to a foundry material known as "Croning" sand. The company claims that the new system makes it possible to produce cast metal parts from CAD data within one day. The system may provide higher accuracy and part complexity than traditional sand-casting. If the surface quality turns out to be good enough, the process may become a serious competitive threat to Soligen's Direct Shell Production Casting.

Two machines are available, EOSINT-S350 and -S700 with build volumes of (340 mm x 340 mm x 590 mm) and (700 mm x 350 mm x 350 mm) respectively. S700 has two scanning heads to speed up the sintering process. The machines have been developed from the company's P-series, originally designed for plastic materials [13,21,24].

DTM LNC-700 This material is a glass filled nylon powder used for the SLS - process. The average particle size is 50 μm enabling features as small as 0.5 mm to be produced. DTM says that the material is the strongest and has the best temperature and chemical resistance of available RP-plastics and that it is therefore especially suitable for making functional prototypes. If paper-adhesive stacks of laminated object manufacturing are ruled out, then it is the first RP-material that is implemented by using the idea of composite materials [27,28].

3.3 FLOOD OF NEW MANUFACTURERS, SOFTWARE SUPPLIERS AND TECHNICAL IMPROVEMENTS

The arrival of new techniques has certainly stimulated the RP-industry. A new market is rapidly developing and expanding which also means intensifying struggles for market share. In practice this means competition based on technical superiority and customer attention, whereas serious price competition is still a way ahead. Rapid prototyping services are available all over the world and RP -manufacturers are found at least in Europe, Middle East, Asia and America. Although RP -units travelling with naval or space explorers are still science fiction, rapid prototyping is well on the way to conquering the world. Below are presented some of the technical improvements which have appeared with the expansion of the field.

All the manufacturers introduced their software improvements in order to make full use of the hardware and to make the system interfaces more user-friendly. In addition to these standard programs, software is supplied for CAD-RP interface improvements and special purposes by third party software developers such as DeskAsters, POGO International and 3D/Eye among others. Comprehensive mapping of this branch of the market would require another book in its own right and therefore the reader is referred to suitable sources such as the annual Rapid Prototyping Directory or Internet home pages [29,30,31]. The list of secondary processes for making short prototype runs is even more extensive, but appropriate information can be found in the reference information at the end of this book [32].

Stereolithography The most important improvement in the field of stereolithography was the introduction of non-toxic materials and cleaning solvents. The new resins brought the safety level and user accessibility of SLA closer to the other rapid prototyping techniques. The first step in the right direction was resins without the carcinogen n-vinyl pyrrolidinone (NVP) [6]. The resins with acrylic are also facing extinction. The latest materials are non-toxic preventing instantaneous health hazards even though the waste resin still needs to be disposed of as problem waste. The improved safety has not affected the development of the mechanical properties of SLA materials [33].

Only laminated object manufacturing can compete with stereolithography for the number of manufacturers. There are at least three manufacturers in Europe, four in Japan and two in the USA. Japanese manufacturers are distinctive in that they allow a much longer development period before entering the market compared to their western counterparts [34]. The material manufacturers are almost as numerous. The number of manufacturers has also meant wide technical diversity which the following examples may illustrate.

In 1995 the biggest SLA manufacturer, 3D Systems, introduced Quick Cast 1.1, an improved version of company's investment casting software. In this version the parts are built with a square interior hatch instead of a triangular one. It also creates a triple skin on any upward or down-facing surface. The new arrangements allow better part drainage and prevent the hatch from damaging the surface skins (and thus the mould surface) during burnout. Quick Cast 1.1 has been reported to have improved significantly the reliability and the part surface quality of the SLA - based investment casting [35,36].

3D Systems released also new, more powerful lasers in order to shorten the build time. They have a laser and optics currently under testing capable of 50 μm diameter spot which could improve the system resolution significantly. The second biggest, EOS GmbH, presented its 'active recoating' resin-applicator and the first solid state lasers in SLA history [27,37]. The Japanese company Mitsui has the only commercial version of the Photocuring Through a Contact Window -process so far.

Laminated Object Manufacturing The cost efficiency and relative technical simplicity of this method encouraged several new companies to introduce their own versions of the idea. Perhaps the most important of these is the Japanese Kira Corp. and their Solid Centre machine with a couple of innovative features: the Solid Centre can use normal copying paper, it has an ink-jet type system to spread the adhesive only where it is needed and a mechanical cutter instead of an expensive laser [38].

Other new LOM-systems are Rapid Prototyping System (RPS) by Kinergy Pte Ltd from Singapore, LaserCAMM by Scale Models Unlimited from USA and JP System 5 (or Shapemaker I & II) by a coalition of the University of Utah and Schroff Development Corp. LaserCAMM has an interesting mode which makes longitudinal and transverse cross-sections of the desired shape. These sections have cuts which are used to fit pieces crosswise to form a large, rough model [40,39].

In response to the competition, Helisys Inc., the first commercial LOM-enterprise, introduced a redesigned version of their LOM-2030 machine. Upgraded subsystems include better X-Y cutting laser controls, Z-lift system, paper feed, fusing system for bonding the sheets of paper and sensors for adjusting lamination pressure and temperature. These improvements make the machine more reliable, more accurate and 30 % faster. In mid-1995 the company released a new High Performance LOM-Paper which should provide better accuracy and building times due to Helisys' new proprietary adhesive [13,27].

Fused Deposition Modelling Perhaps the most important of Stratasys Inc.'s novelties is easier support removal. The new dual-nozzle system enables the depositing of a layer of 'release material' between a support and the part. The arrangement prevents damage to parts during cleaning. New head design provides a better surface finish, finer detail and higher material flow rate. One of the new

3.3 FLOOD OF NEW MANUFACTURERS, SOFTWARE   29

materials is Medical ABS, which can withstand gamma sterilisation. Stratasys have also purchased the FDM -technology which IBM had been developing. As part of the transaction IBM became a 15 % shareholder of Stratasys. The new know-how and extended ownership may bear fruit in the near future [41].

Solid Ground Curing Cubital is one of the few companies which reduced its system prices during the project period. At the end of 1994, the newly introduced SOLIDER 4600 included several other improvements. It allows the user to define layer thickness between 76 and 203 µm. The build volume is also adjustable to minimise material consumption and delivery time. Improved ionographic cartridge - CT2010 - provides better mask image quality and thus accuracy. The unit itself is upgradable to SOLIDER 5600.

Cubital has also refined the SGC-process sequence. The old cycle exposed the layer to the high-intensity UV-light right after the removal of the uncured resin. Thus a thin "skin" of cured resin was produced between the wax layers. The new arrangement post-cures the layer at the end of the cycle. At this stage of the cycle the support wax has already been solidified and the layer has been milled to the desired thickness. In this manner a thin layer of uncured resin is left between the layers of support wax thus easing up the part cleanup. The new building process cycle reduces the time needed for part cleanup and does not require citric acid in de-waxing. The post processing time can be minimised with the new de-waxing machine. The low-shrinkage material X7501, designed for the new build process, is more durable and flexible allowing snap fit assemblies and functional models.

In addition to the refinements of the conventional build cycle, Cubital introduced new Extended Solid Ground Curing Process for production of parts out of thermoset, thermoplastic and metallic materials. Instead of creating a cross-section of the part and surrounding it with support material, the new cycle forms a cavity of the required shape with photocuring support material. The cavity is then filled with build material and the layer is milled normally. The build material does not necessarily have to be UV-curable. The company has plans to introduce metal and ceramic materials for ESGC during 1996. SGC technology can be used to make metal parts even now: a German company Schneider Prototyping GmbH claims that through their Cubital-based SoliCast process they can provide metal prototypes inexpensively in two weeks [27,42].

Direct Shell Production Casting Formerly Soligen Inc., instead of selling RP-units, sold only licences including the machine and unlimited warranty. To get an unit at their disposal, the licensees paid the basic license and a fee based on usage. In 1995 the company continued its unusual marketing approaches by introducing the Parts Now -strategy. Parts Now allows the customer to procure custom metal parts via the Interment. Slogan says that by combining DSc, CNN-machining and traditional casting they can provide the first metal parts within five working days after receiving the appropriate CAD-files. The cost of the parts is determined primarily by size, not shape [43].

3.4 MAJOR RESEARCH DIRECTIONS

As mentioned above, none of the present rapid prototyping techniques are able to fully satisfy customer demand. Therefore, both the development of existing methods and the hunt for new ones is continuous. In addition to the search for better accuracy the major trends in research seem to be aimed at improving the material properties and the development of cheaper design verification RP-units. Research is not restricted solely to RP-oriented enterprises. New technology may open new opportunities not only in product development but also in material research and manufacturing [4].

3.4.1 Development of existing systems

Droplet deposition manufacturing 3D Systems, the largest RP-producer, published the first information about its own version of the idea in the fall 1995. The technology of company's first non-stereolithography unit is called Multi-Jet Modeling (MJM) and the new machine itself Office Modeler. As the name hints, the machine is intended to be used in offices for design verifications. In this sense it is a rival to BPM's Personal Modeler. At the time of writing available technical data was rather ambiguous because the company had not fixed the production model specifications. The following is drawn from a combination of different sources and may deviate from the final established configuration.

The system deposits thermoplastic material in successive layers with a print head consisting of 96 jets oriented in a 2.5 inch wide linear array. The jets shoot the material in 76 µm diameter droplets and are cleaned automatically after each part-building cycle. The number of jets renders possible a build rate twice as fast as that of the company's stereolithography units. To support the overhangs the machine creates a forest of very thin hairs of build material on the underside. The supports are removed simply by sweeping the fibres off. Neither special tools nor chemicals are needed in the part clean-up.

Removal of the supports leaves the undersides rough, but otherwise the surface finish is said to be sufficient at least for concept verifications. Accurate X-Y-positioning and the droplet size enables the system to reproduce fine details. At the time of the writing the material itself is also under development in order to improve the speed of the process and to remove the tacky feel of the parts. It is presumed

3.4 MAJOR RESEARCH DIRECTIONS

that the material will not be strong enough to be used in secondary reproducing processes such as investment casting. Improving the speed of the process is higher in the company's priorities than strength of the material because the Office Modeler is intended to allow designers a chance to evaluate early design concepts at will. The prototypes for the functional tests and the secondary processes are undertaken by the company's SLA-units. The average price of parts is predicted to be US$5-30.

The machine's size is most accurately described by comparison with a "medium size floor-standing copy machine". It is quiet, it does not require any special air-conditioning or cooling systems and runs on normal network current. The company claims that the advanced control software and the process reliability makes it as easy to use and maintain as average paper printers. The user should be free from concerns about part orientation, defected STL-files, build parameters or support generation. The machine uses a TCP/IP interface to connect directly onto computer networks. Commercial release is expected during 1996. The technical similarity may lead the company into a patent conflict with Sanders and BPM, similar to the quarrel between EOS GmbH and 3D Systems [26,44].

There are several other companies that have been interested in this technique. At least Incre Inc. (under process name Incremental fabrication), the University of California (Precision Droplet Stream Manufacturing Technology) and Micro Fab Inc. (Solder Jet -system) have been studying the possibility of making parts out of metals with low melting points such as tin and aluminium. Texas Instruments has been developing a multi-jet array system under the names Printed Computer Tomography and Protojet 3D [38].

Of these companies Incre has bought rights to BPM's patents. It has also been able to exhibit some simple and rough parts made of tin and aluminium. MicroFab originally developed its 60 µm tin droplet technology in order to print two-dimensional electronic circuits [6,45].

Laminated Object Manufacturing At the 1995 Dayton rapid prototyping conference Helisys Inc. released preliminary information on their first non-paper based material since the introduction of the LOM -system. The new material is a polyester plastic similar to that used to manufacture large soft-drink bottles. It is much stronger than current paper material and does not suffer from the problems of moisture absorption and subsequent swelling. The company says that existing Helisys machines should not require modifications in order to use the new material. The price has been estimated to be 18 - 26 US$/kg (current paper material costs 7 US$/kg) [30].

In AUTOFACT '95 the company had samples of their new fibre-reinforced composite on display. This does not absorb moisture and is said to have extremely high tensile strength and temperature resistance. Both materials will be commercially available during 1996 [13].

Selectively-Coloured Stereolithography Models As a result of the Brite-Euram project PHIDIAS (laser Photopolymerisation models based in medical Imaging; a Development Improving the Accuracy of Surgery) a British company Zeneca Specialities has developed a stereolithography resin that can be dyed at desired locations of the model with extra radiation. Special additives in the resin generate colour when exposed to a dose of UV-light in excess of the normal build cycle radiation. The material can be used with either helium-cadmium or argon lasers.

The resin is developed mainly for medical purposes and can help in visualising the 3D scans of organs, tumours etc. The finished parts are mostly transparent with the highlighted areas either opaque blue or red. Other colours are under development. According to the company the material is non-toxic and can even be used in an operation room as a template during surgery.

Another consortium member, a third party software developer, Materialise, N.V. from Belgium sells the MIMICS/CT-Modeler software capable of converting computer tomography (CT) and magnetic resonance imaging (MRI) data to a format suitable for RP-units. The program allows the user to highlight the desired parts of the image and then calculates the control code for the SLA unit. After each normal layer building cycle the regions intended to be coloured are re-scanned at a lower speed in order to provide a sufficient UV dose. The resin should become commercially available during the first quarter of 1996 [13,46].

Light Sculpting This is the very first technique that was used to provide commercial rapid prototyping services. In the original version the parts are built on a platform descending into a vat of liquid photo-polymer resin. Layers are cured with an UV lamp through a series of photo-plotted masks set, one by one, on a glass plate. This contact window is placed on the surface of the resin so that the part is not in contact with air. Because each layer is cured through the corresponding mask, the layer complexity or resolution does not affect the building time.

On the same side of the window as the resin a layer of halogenic compound, such as Teflon, inhibits the curing of the topmost surface of each layer and thus prevents the part from being attached to the window. Similarly, an uncured region on the top of each layer is also formed in the normal stereolithography process due to the presence of inhibiting oxygen. This sub-layer has an important role in promoting the attachment of new layers because it allows proper cross-linking between the new layer and the part. However, Teflon is a much milder inhibitor than oxygen and therefore the required energy for curing is much smaller in the

3.4 MAJOR RESEARCH DIRECTIONS 33

Light Sculpting process. This enables the use of less expensive radiation sources than a laser [6].

Inventor Efrem Fudim has now developed the system further and removed the resin vat. The upgraded version has simply a system that spreads a layer of resin on the underside of the glass contact window. The new layer is partially cured before it is brought into contact with the part and affixed to it with further radiation. The improved procedure minimises warpage because the completed layers are not over-cured by excess radiation.

Each layer takes about 30 seconds to make and the layer thickness can be varied to maximise the speed/accuracy ratio. Masks are printed in a separate printer and loaded onto the build unit which changes them automatically. The printer can make sixteen (216 mm × 280 mm) -sized masks per minute. The masks cost 20 cents each and can be reused to produce duplicates.

Fudim has now decided to start selling machines instead of just offering RP-services and is looking for investors to enter the market. A small (1070 mm × 700 mm × 790 mm[wdh]) unit with (300 mm × 300 mm × 300 mm) build volume would cost about US$105 000 including the mask printer, custom slicing software, 23 litres of resin and a two-year warranty [34].

Photocuring through a contact window Besides Light Sculpting Inc., Milwaukee, only Japanese manufacturers have been interested in utilising the benefits of a contact window. Mitsui Engineering & Ship Building sells COLAMM equipment where the resin is cured with a laser through a descending contact window. The part and the supports hang on the top of the vat. Although the Japanese RP-market has been a bit stagnant due to the lack of 3D CAD-systems the research has not stopped. In addition to the development of conventional systems new openings have also been made [6,34].

For example the University of Tokyo and the Kyushu Institute of Technology have been studying the possibilities of microstereolithography. Using either a laser or the highly-focused beam of a xenon lamp these groups have managed to produce photopolymer structures with dimensions below 100 µm. The system resolution has been 5 µm at its best. The Tokyo team has also carried out experiments with metal and ceramic microparts (see next paragraph).

The Kyushu team has developed a conducting photopolymer. By using this they have built a micro-electrostatic actuator as small as (120 µm × 50 µm × 700 µm) They call the technique 'integrated hardened polymer stereolithography', IH. The problems of microstereolithography resemble the ones on the macro-scale: inhomogeneities and viscous effects of the resin as well as part adhesion to the contact window [38,47].

Solid phase with SLA-resins The limited strength of the material has always restricted the use of stereolithography parts. To improve the part durability several composite structures have been suggested. Clemson University has developed an experimental unit which automates the placement of long fibres into the resin. Continuous fibre, which is made of material transparent to UV light (such as glass or quartz), is laid down on the top of the vat to fit the cross-section of the part. Extra time to allow the fibre to be wetted is needed before the layer can be cured. Even the transparent solid phase prevents light from penetrating the part and thus inhibits curing. The resulting parts have highly anisotropic properties because the fibres do not promote layer adhesion [48].

Better isotropy of properties could be achieved by using short fibres. However, short fibres do not remove shadowing and special means are required to achieve a homogeneous distribution of fibres. Because the short fibres would be randomly oriented, the fibres protruding from the part's surface might cause problems if the part is used in secondary processes. Removing these fibres requires extra labour and causes annoying dust. On the other hand the protruding fibres would enhance the adhesion of any possible coating. The most interesting short fibres are whiskers. For example aluminium borate whiskers have sufficient chemical resistance to be used with different photopolymer resins. High thermal resistance renders it possible to use them also in other RP-processes. Working with whiskers requires special precautions to avoid health hazards [49,50].

The University of Tokyo, in co-operation with Olympus Ltd., has been studying the production of micro size metal and ceramic parts. In their method particles with an average diameter of 0.25 - 3 µm are dispensed evenly in the photopolymer resin by several hours of ultrasonic vibration treatment. The parts are cured with He-Cad laser through a contact window. Parts are then taken to an oven, the binder is burned away at 300 - 500 °C and sintered at approximately 1000 °C. The team has made some simple shapes with dimensions below 30 µm. Although some problems in binder burn-out and sintering have been reported, the powder-resin composites are stronger than conventional ones [51].

Similar experiments on the macro-scale have been made at the University of Michigan with resins into which silica or alumina powders have been dispensed. One of the project's objectives is to find out whether 'green' ceramic parts can be made with stereolithography. So far successful experiments have been carried out with 60 % silica solutions [30].

Selective Laser Sintering DTM Corp. is working continuously with the University of Texas to improve the available selection of SLS-materials. They have performed experiments with dual phase metals, binder coated ceramics, HIP-method and nanophase materials. Interesting examples are the bone-like materials calcium hydroxyapatite and calcium phosphate which may be used in medical

3.4 MAJOR RESEARCH DIRECTIONS

applications. Selective laser sintering of materials with high melting points is also under study at least in the Fraunhofer Institute in Aachen and in the University of Stuttgart [18,19,52].

Selective Laser Reactive Sintering (SLRS) offers interesting perspectives on expanding the material selection available. It is a method where powder reacts with another substance during sintering and forms the final part material. Usually the reaction takes place between the powder and surrounding gas or two powder constituents. For example a carbon containing gas reacts with silicon to form silicon carbide. The technique has been used to produce several other oxides, nitrides and carbides. If the surrounding atmosphere is used to deposit material in order to bind the particles together only, the method is called Selective Area Laser Deposition with Vapor Infiltration (SALDVI). It is used mainly in micro-scale applications [53,54,55].

Fused Deposition Modeling with metals and ceramics Fraunhofer Institute for Applied Materials Research (IFAM) and Fraunhofer Institute for Manufacturing Engineering and Automation (IPA) have been developing the Multiphase Jet Solidification (MJS) method similar to Stratasys' FDM. The object of the project is to provide a method for making parts directly out of metal and ceramic materials. The group has made experiments with a tin-bismuth alloy which is commonly used in metal spraying. The extrusion of the molten alloy has not caused problems but due to the low viscosity the accuracy and the part complexity have been limited. Experiments to mix alloying particles into the metal in order to increase viscosity have shown promising results.

The Fraunhofer team has also performed experiments where metals with high melting points or ceramic powder has been mixed with the plastic binder. The extrusion of such mixture is very accurate due to the low surface tension. The 'green' part can be easily finished before the binder is dissolved and the part is sintered. The shrinkage is approximately 30 % during sintering. The sintering can also be done only partially and then the resulting porous model infiltrated with a lower-melting point alloy or epoxy [56].

The University of Arizona and Advanced Ceramics Research Company have together tested a method where thermally curable resin, loaded with ceramic particles, is lead through a nozzle to a heated environment where the resin is cured. The 'green' part is built as in the normal FDM-process and then placed in an oven where the binder is burned away and the part is sintered. The method has also been tested with short carbon fibres resin [45].

3D Printing In this method the desired shape is printed with the binder on to successive layers of powder-like raw material. The binder ties the powder particles and layers together and the resulting 'green' part is placed in an oven and sintered. The method is already used commercially by Soligen Inc. under the name Direct Shell Production Casting. Soligen uses it in the direct production of ceramic investment casting shells. The inventor of the technique, Massachusetts Institute of Technology, has been studying the possibilities of making metal, functional ceramic and composite parts with it. In order to make 3D Printing a viable RP-method in the tightening business situation, MIT has been obliged to improve part accuracy.

In addition to the normal stair-stepping in the Z-direction, the raster deposition of the binder material leaves horizontal step-like pattern at the layer edges due to the different lengths of adjacent raster lines. MIT's answer to this problem is called proportional defection. It allows the deviation of the electronically charged droplet stream in order to smooth the roughness of the layer edges. The surface quality may be further improved by minimising powder surface distortion due to the impact of the drops and the blurring caused by the binder diffusion [47,57,58].

Successor of the STL-file format Speculation on the successor to the present de facto standard RP-interface is becoming more and more topical. With increasing system accuracy the demand for higher fidelity to the original design is becoming real. Because of the STL-standard's model representation structure, based on triangles, the better design fidelity and resolution means impractical large file-sizes. The new standard should also take into account potential future needs such as part colours, materials and the possibility of new RP-methods that do not rely directly on manufacturing in layers. Perhaps due to the simplicity and generality of the STL format several sceptical opinions of the benefits of breaking the status quo have been expressed.

Programs capable of converting CAD-models directly to the RP-unit control code are provided by Fockele & Schwarze GmbH and Sanders Prototype Inc among others. This type of program has questioned the need for a STL-file or some other corresponding intermediate stage between the design computer and a RP-unit. The direct slicing of CAD-data removes one time-consuming step and prevents possible errors in file conversion. Suggestions for a contour based standard which are already commercial are for example LEAF by the Helsinki University of Technology, Common Layer Interface (CLI) by Brite-EuRam RPT-project and Contour Tools developed by Materialise in Brite-EuRam Phidias-project [3,59,60,61].

3.4.2 New approaches and horizons

Three Dimensional Welding Since the German steel company Thyssen AG ceased to use the Shape Welding-method for manufacturing large industrial components in 1985, there has not been any commercial RP-activity based on three

3.4 MAJOR RESEARCH DIRECTIONS

dimensional welding. In the Thyssen method an array of welding heads deposited the build metal into the desired shape on a pre-shaped mandrel. The system was intended to be used for the manufacturing of large pressure vessels and turbine shafts for the nuclear and petrochemical industries.

Because of the possibility to manufacture solid metal parts directly and the potential for using exotic alloys the methods excite continuous interest. In the early 1980's, an American company, Babcock & Wilcox Co. developed seriously an arc-welding method called Shape Melting, but seems to have lost interest since. In Europe developments have been concentrated in the United Kingdom. Rolls Royce and the Universities of Nottingham and Cranfield have studied MIG-welding as a potential manufacturing method. B & W has produced prototypes of heavy industrial pipeline components whereas Nottingham and Cranfield have experimented with smaller parts such as functional car engine part prototypes. The exhibited parts have been rather robust with a distinctive coiled appearance [6,57].

Laser generating is practically another three dimensional welding method. Instead of arc welding, laser generating uses a focused laser beam to fuse powder-like build material to the part surface. The build material is fed directly to the laser spot with a powder jet. The only restrictions on the material are set by material reflectivity and laser power. The method has been developed from a laser surface treating method called cladding. The resolution of the system is defined mainly by the laser spot size.

At the moment laser generating research is done at Los Alamos National Laboratory, Fraunhofer Institute for Production Technology (IPT) and the University of Stuttgart. The Los Alamos team calls the method Directed Light Fabrication (DLF) and Fraunhofer researchers use the name Laser Aided Powder Solidification with Jet (LAPS-J). The researchers in Fraunhofer and Stuttgart have been testing the system simultaneously with the SLS of materials with high melting points [19,52].

So far the published results have been rather promising. The Fraunhofer team has presented cylinders, cones and turbine blade profiles made out of stainless steel and copper. The wall thickness achieved have been between 0.5 and 0.7 mm. The Los Alamos team has also produced parts with simple shapes in the size of a 76 mm cube. Materials used have been stainless steel, tungsten, nickel aluminides, molybdenum disilicide and aluminium. The team claims that the system is accurate to within "a few thousands of an inch" [59,62].

Metal spraying is commonly used in processes where RP-parts are reproduced or strengthened to make prototype tooling. It is suitable for use with rapid models because of the relatively low deposition temperature. Several propositions have been made for the direct use of metal spraying in the part making. None of these has reached the commercial stage and the interest has faded recently.

MD* Shape Deposition of the Carnegie Mellon University is perhaps the most advanced RP-concept using metal spraying. The prototype system sprays the build metal through disposable masks to the substrate. After each cross section has been sprayed the sacrificial support material is sprayed with a complementary mask exposing the unsprayed areas. Masks are cut from pressure-sensitive labelling paper with a CO_2 laser. One of the benefits of the system mentioned has been the possibility of using multiple materials and building electro-mechanical assemblies directly [57].

According to some sources Stanford University in California has also been developing a similar system called Shape Deposition Modeling. Instead of masks the thermally deposited layers are shaped with a 5-axis CNC machine and then shot-peened to remove internal stresses. The University of Exeter, UK has experimented with spraying metal through a modified artist's air brush. The air brush forms a nozzle which allows the metal spray to be directed accurately. Using a low temperature melting (58°C) alloy of bismuth, lead and tin they have made simple cylinder shaped parts with 1.0mm - 1.4mm wall thickness [63].

Metal sheet methods The University of Dundee has been working on two different methods for making parts out of stainless steel sheets. The first is a LOM-like method where laser-cut cross sections are stacked and attached to each other by welding, soldering or gluing. Heavy staircasing and the bonding between layers require further development.

The other method is Laser Forming. When a suitably powered laser tracks over a sheet of metal following the desired path, the top surface of the bend line melts while the lower surface is left almost unaffected. When the upper surface cools, it contracts and bends the sheet at the bend line. By repeating this procedure the desired angle can be reached. Even 2mm thick steel plates can be bent the full 90 degrees without mechanical interruption. Curved shapes are also possible, but warpage may then become a problem [64].

Micro and nanomechanics Although rapid prototyping has become a serious branch of industry, the micro- and nanoscale still remains an open space for visionaries to conquer. Micro-robots repairing nerves and an army of miniature nanofactories controlling a chemical process may serve as examples. To date the achievements in micro-scale have been impressive. For example the computer on which this text was written is a result of long and successful work with micro-lithography. Unfortunately the present micro-methods are designed for mass production and need huge investments. The operation in only two dimensions is another shortcoming. To make the dreams come true, scientists have begun to combine micro-lithography with different applications of Laser Chemical Vapor Deposition (LCVD), particle beam manipulation and photocuring through a contact window. Silicon, familiar as it is, is a promising material for micro-machines because it is stronger than steel and it can be made semiconducting by selective doping. There is also a lot of experience of handling it. LCVD has made it possible to experiment with exotic materials like tungsten and diamond. The aim is to develop Micro Electro Mechanical Systems (MEMS) and automate their production. Tiny machines can be much more efficient than their giant counterparts because they do not suffer inertial forces and their functional resolution is better [6,47,53].

3.5 REFERENCES

[1] Rapid Prototyping Report, The newsletter of the desktop manufacturing industry, July 1995, *CAD/CAM Publishing Inc., 1010 Turquoise Street, Suite #320, San Diego, California 92109, USA*

[2] Ref. [1], Dec. 1994

[3] Ref. [1], May 1994

[4] Terry Wohlers, *Future potential of rapid prototyping and manufacturing around the world*, Rapid Prototyping Journal, Vol. 1, Number 1, 1995, MCB Univ. Press Ltd.

[5] Ref. [1], April 1994

[6] Marshall Burns, *Automated Fabrication, Improving productivity in manufacturing*, PTR Prentice Hall, Englewood Cliffs, New Jersey 07632, USA

[7] Al Hastbacka, Sanders Prototype Inc. president, *Personal communications*

[8] Ref. [1], March 1994

[9] Al Hastbacka, Sanders Prototype Inc. president, *Personal communications, rp-ml@cs.hut.fi*

[10] Model Maker, Desktop 3D Modeling System, *Sanders Prototype Inc. information brochure, Autofact'95 RP-conference*

[11] Model Maker, Application Note #1-3 *Sanders Prototype Inc. information brochure, Dearborn 1995 RP-conference*

[12] Ref. [1], April 1995

[13] Ref. [1], Dec. 1995

[14] Roger P. Orban, BPM technologies Inc., *Personal communications, rp-ml@cs.hut.fi*

[15] Herbert E. Menhennett, Vice President and Director of Engineering, BPM Technology Inc., *Personal Modelling Office Machine*, Rapid News, Volume 3, Number 2, Advanced Technology Centre, Warwick Manufacturing Group, University of Warwick, Coventry, UK, June 1995

[16] A 21st Century Technology...Today, *BPM Technology Inc. information brochure, Oct. 20 1995, Patrick Lanfear, National Sales Manager*

[17] W.D. Kingery, H.K. Bowen, D.R. Uhlmann, *Introduction to Ceramics, 2nd edition*, John Wiley & Sons, Canada, 1976

[18] Harris L. Marcus, David Bourell, A. Manthiram, Joseph Beaman, Joel Barlow, Richard Crawford, Laser Processed Freeform Fabrication, *Proceedings of the 3rd European Conference on Rapid Prototyping and Manufacturing*, Edited by Dr P.M.Dickens, The University of Nottingham, Quorn Litho, Loughborough, Leicestershire LE11 1HH, 1994

[19] Thomas Lück, Frithjof Baumann, Bernd Keller, Bernd Wiedemann, Material Research and Development for Rapid Prototyping Techniques at the IKP, *Proceedings of the 3rd European Conference on Rapid Prototyping and Manufacturing*, Edited by Dr P.M.Dickens, The University of Nottingham, Quorn Litho, Loughborough, Leicestershire LE11 1HH, 1994

[20] European patent specification, WO 90/1185 18.10.90 Gazette 90/24, *O.Nyrhilä, S.Syrjälä*

[21] Olli Nyrhilä, Project Manager, Electrolux Rapid Development, *Personal communications*

3.5 REFERENCES

[22] Seppo Syrjälä, Project Manager, Electrolux Rapid Development, *Personal communications*

[23] Veli-Matti Tiainen, *The Present State and Future Prospects of Rapid Prototyping, Master's Thesis (in Finnish),* The University of Helsinki, 1996

[24] Making Light Work, Solutions for Rapid Prototyping, *Electro Optical Systems information brochure*, 12/95

[25] Ref. [1], Sept. 1995

[26] Ref. [1], Nov. 1995

[27] Rapid News, Volume 3, Number 2, Advanced Technology Centre, Warwick Manufacturing Group, University of Warwick, Coventry, UK, June 1995

[28] Ref. [1], March 1995

[29] The Rapid Prototyping Directory, *CAD/CAM Publishing Inc., 1010 Turquoise Street, Suite #320, San Diego, California 92109, USA*

[30] Ref. [1], June 1995

[31] Rapid Prototyping mailing list, *rp-ml@cs.hut.fi]*

[32] Layer Manufacturing - A Challenge of the Future *Nordisk Industrifond*, Edited by Professor Öyvind Björke, Tapir Publishers, Trondheim, Norway, 1992

[33] Paul F. Jacobs, Ph.D., *Rapid Prototyping & Manufacturing - Fundamentals of Stereolithography,* Society of Manufacturing Engineers, One SME Drive, P.O. Box 930, Dearborn, MI 48121-0930, USA, 1992

[34] Ref. [1], Oct. 1995

[35] Paul F. Jacobs, Director of Research and Development, 3D Systems Corp., *Quick Cast -book, preliminary information, in preparation 1996*

[36] Jukka Tuomi, Project Manager, Helsinki University of Technology, Lahti Centre, *Personal communications*

[37] Ref. [1], Aug. 1994

[38] Ref. [1], July 1994

[39] William Leichter. LaserCAMM, *Rapid Prototyping with Laser Cutting*, Dearborn 1995 RP-conference presentation notes

[40] Ref. [1], May 1995

[41] Jim Fendrick, Vice President, International sales, Stratasys Inc. *FDM Update*, Autofact'95 RP-conference presentation notes

[42] Yehudah Baron, Cubital America Inc. *Process Refinement/System Update*, Dearborn 1995 RP-conference presentation notes

[43] Soligen Technologies Inc., *World-Wide Web, http://www.partsnow.com*

[44] Technology Brief, *3D Systems information brochure, Autofact'95 RP-conference*

[45] Ref. [1], Sept. 1993

[46] Dr. Kevin McAloon, Dr. Martin R. Edwards, Ajay H. Popat, Zeneca Specialities, *Selectively-Coloured Stereolithography Models*, European Action on Rapid Prototyping, No. 7, Dec. 1995, Denmark

[47] Ref. [1], Jan. 1994

[48] Thierry Renault, Amod A. Ogale, Processing of Fiber Reinfoced Resins in an Automated Desktop Photolithography Unit, *Proceedings of the 3rd European Conference on Rapid Prototyping and Manufacturing*, Edited by Dr P.M.Dickens, The University of Nottingham, Quorn Litho, Loughborough, Leicestershire LE11 1HH, 1994

[49] Shikoku Chemicals Corp., Aluminum Borate Whisker - Alborex, Patent pending

[50] Assoc. prof. Reijo Lappalainen, the University of Helsinki, Department of Physics, *Personal communications*

[51] Ref. [1], Feb. 1995

3.5 REFERENCES

[52] W. König, T. Celiker, Y.-A. Song, Rapid Prototyping of Metallic Parts, *Proceedings of the 3rd European Conference on Rapid Prototyping and Manufacturing*, Edited by Dr P.M.Dickens, The University of Nottingham, Quorn Litho, Loughborough, Leicestershire LE11 1HH, 1994

[53] University of Texas, *http://shimano.me.utexas.edu/sff/sls.html*

[54] Kamatchi Subramanian, Neal Vail, Joel Barlow, Harris Marcus, *Selective laser sintering of alumina with polymer binder*, Rapid Prototyping Journal, Vol. 1, Number 2, 1995, MCB Univ. Press Ltd.

[55] Mukesh Agarwala, David Bourell, Joseph Beaman, Harris Marcus, Joel Barlow, *Post-processing of selective laser sintered metal parts*, Rapid Prototyping Journal, Vol. 1, Number 2, 1995, MCB Univ. Press Ltd.

[56] Michael Greulich, Matthias Greul, Theo Pintat, *Fast, functional prototypes via multiphase jet solidification*, Rapid Prototyping Journal, Vol. 1, Number 1, 1995, MCB Univ. Press Ltd.

[57] Manufacturing Technology Information Analysis Center (MTIAC), *http://www.dtic.dla.mil/iac/mtiac/RP44.HTML*

[58] Massachusetts Institute of Technology, *http://web.mit.edu/asf/athena/org/t/tdp/www/home.html*

[59] Ref. [1], Jan. 1995

[60] Common Layer Interface, Brite EuRam project BE5930, *http://www.cranfield.ac.uk*

[61] Wilfried Vancraen, Bart Swaelens, Johan Pauwels, Contour Interfacing in Rapid Prototyping - Tools that Make It Work, *Proceedings of the 2nd European Conference on Rapid Prototyping and Manufacturing*, Edited by Dr P.M.Dickens, The University of Nottingham, Quorn Litho, Loughborough, Leicestershire LE11 1HH, 1994

[62] F. Klocke, T. Celiker, Y.-A. Song, *Rapid metal tooling*, Rapid Prototyping Journal, Vol. 1, Number 3, 1995, MCB Univ. Press Ltd.

[63] J. Bryant, M. A. Jenkins, Sprayed Metal Deposition, *Proceedings of the 2nd European Conference on Rapid Prototyping and Manufacturing*, Edited by

Dr P.M.Dickens, The University of Nottingham, Quorn Litho, Loughborough, Leicestershire LE11 1HH, 1993

[64] Gareth A. Thompson, Mark S. Pridham, The Use of a High Powered Laser Machining Centre in the Production of Metal Prototypes, *Proceedings of the 2nd European Conference on Rapid Prototyping and Manufacturing*, Edited by Dr P. M. Dickens, The University of Nottingham, Quorn Litho, Loughborough, Leicestershire LE11 1HH, 1994

4 DESIGN METHODOLOGY

4.1 INTRODUCTION

With the market introduction of the Stereolithography apparatus in the year 1987, a new technology had emerged. The idea of building parts by an incremental layer technique seemed so attractive that the development of a lot of other technological groups were initiated. Except for chemical solidification of liquid photopolymers, these were melting techniques using NC-controlled nozzles, ink-jet printing heads and laser sintering of powders, deposition of binders to powder layers and the thermal cutting and lamination of solid sheet materials.

In this first "founding" phase of the *Rapid Prototyping Technique*, a lot of people were euphoric about these technologies; suddenly, everything seemed possible.

Then came a second phase of disillusion, as practical limitations turned out. The accuracy and the material properties of the parts did not reach the values of conventionally manufactures objects, and still doesn't. Independently from the technology, *Rapid Prototyping* started to be regarded as a basic method of product development.

Now we are in the third phase - the manufacturing technology. The accuracy and material limitations as well as the user-friendliness improved, process chains for conversion of RP parts to various target materials emerged. Now, the *Rapid Product Development* is used more often. This expression reflects the idea that product development concepts like Rapid Prototyping and Reverse Engineering *and* methods like Concurrent Engineering, Quality Function Deployment and others can be considered as supplementary tools aiming at better and cheaper products brought into market with a shorter lead time.

4.2 CHANGING REQUIREMENTS IN PRODUCT DEVELOPMENT AND MANUFACTURING

4.2.1 Changed Requirements for the Manufacturing Industry

In the 90's a short development time -time to market- will be one of the most decisive competition parameters to the manufacturing industry.

The requirements from the market have changed drastically in many ways through the 70's and 80's. To survive in the still more competitive market you must offer your products in a large number of variants, containing highly sophisticated functions without compromising the delivery time (see Figure 4.1).

As a kind of contrast to these values, which have been put into the product through the development process one must realise, that the average lifetime has decreased through the same period (see Figure 4.2).

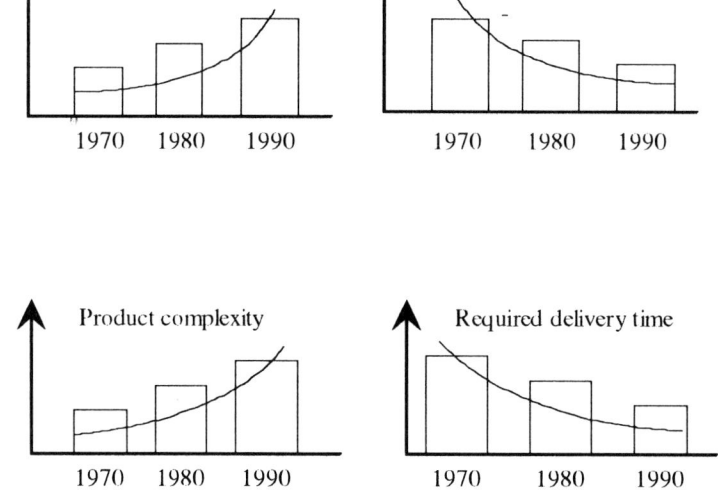

Figure 4.1. Changed Requirements for the Manufacturing Industry.

4.2 CHANGING REQUIREMENTS

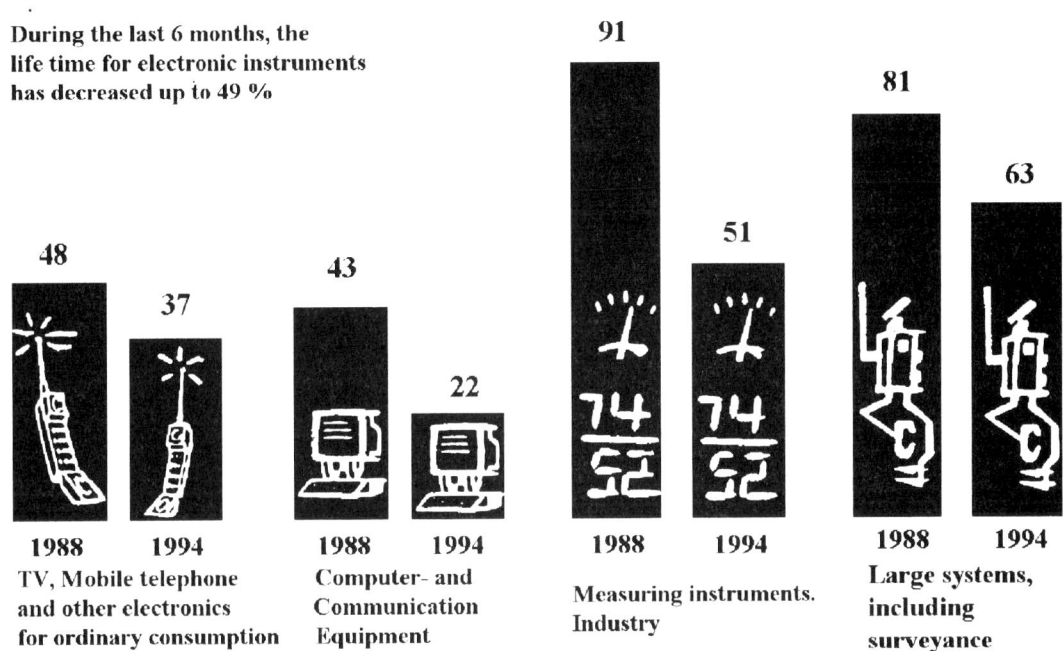

Figure 4.2. Decrease in Product Lifetime of Electronic Industry.

These statements are based upon a great number of surveys and analysis carried out in the middle 80's and comparing the situation in the EU, the Far East and the United States, main focus being placed upon the car industry.

All experiences indicate, that this evolution will continue through the 90's, in which fact you will find an explanation why so much focus is placed on the development phase.

At the same time one has to consider that:

- of the quality of a product is created in the development phase
- of the costs of a product is decided in the product development function
- months delay in the introduction of the product to the market may reduce the total lifetime-profit with more than 30%

These figures underline the importance of the *Product Development Function* to the competitive power of your company. This importance is further emphasised by Figure 4.3 and 4.4.

Does shorter delivery time and better services mean bigger costs? No, -the shorter lead time and the better service may be acquired through rational and efficient systems and working methods as well as utilisation of advanced tools, - like RPT.

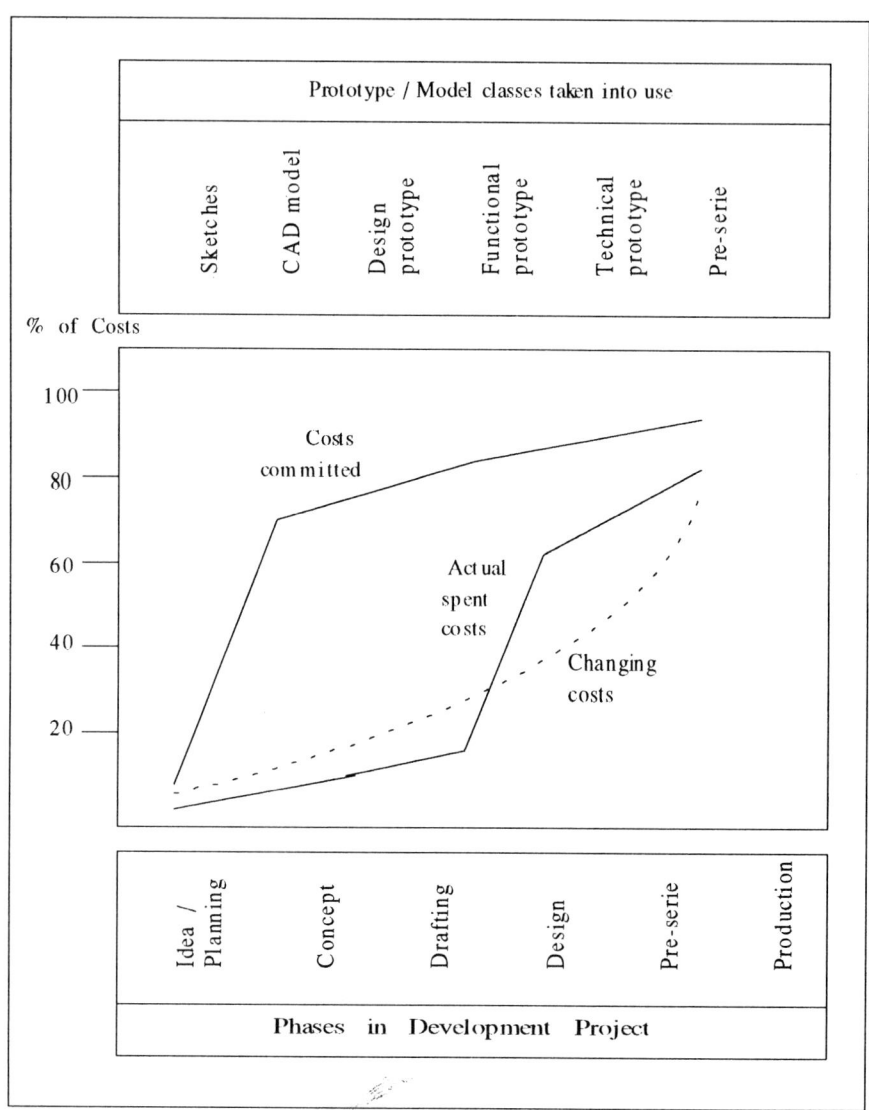

Figure 4.3. Committed, Spent and Changing Costs in Different Phases in a Development Process.

4.2 CHANGING REQUIREMENTS

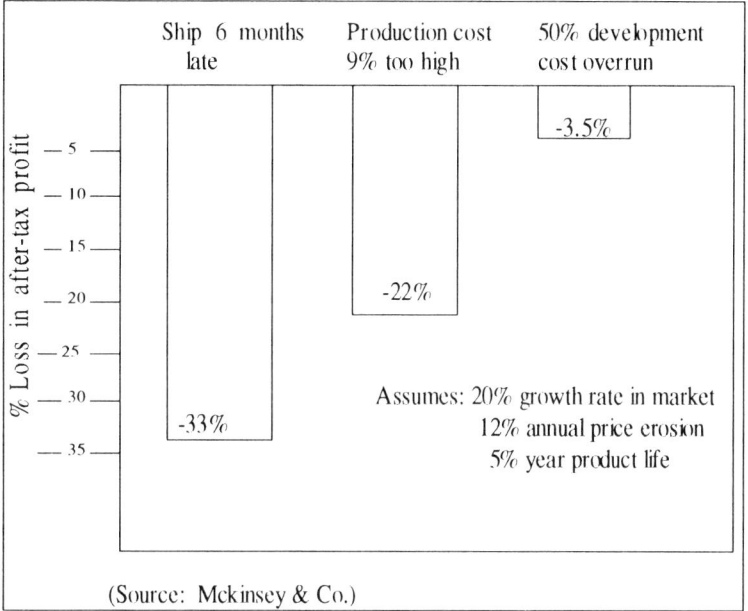

Figure 4.4. The Influence of an Overrun in the Development Cost is Negligible, Compared with the Loss in Profit due to a Delay in Shipment or too High Production Costs.

4.2.2 Influence of RTP on Competition Parameters

Which are the competition parameters and how may they be influenced?

- Time-to-Market
- Aesthetic appearance
- Flexibility
- Quality
- Price

Most of these parameters may be influenced through use of new technologies. Talking in particular about Rapid Prototyping it is a fact, that the more availability of reliable prototypes, leads to fewer iteration cycles, and thus cheaper development of higher-quality products. These advantages are common to most classes of prototypes, whether they are physical or virtual.

Time-to-Market as a Competition Parameter
More and more of our leading companies stress TIME as a significant source to create competition benefits. The main difference between growing and non-growing companies is [G.Ø] the way TIME is handled in product development,

production, distribution, sales and administration, -in other words: in all parts of the company.

Growing companies are able to:

- Supply products in shorter time than their competitors
- Develop and launch new products faster than their competitors
- Reduce lead-time in the company faster than their competitors.

A Finnish producer of windows has, according to [G.Ø] delivery time for a specific type of windows of six days, whereas his competitors operate with a delivery time of six weeks -for the same type of windows.

The delivery time of another company producing customer specified doors for industry (in principle an infinite number of types) is three to four weeks where the normal delivery time in the trade is three to four months.

During the last years, Electrolux Cleaning Service in Vestervik, Sweden, which produces engines for 200 different types of vacuum cleaners, has improved the lead-time 40 times, and are able to supply the customer with the model he wants within three days. Quality has been improved and quality costs have been reduced with 87%. The production of engines has been moved to Sweden in spite of the fact that Swedish wages are higher. Delivery times are, however, shorter and costs lower than those of the competitors.

Companies who are able to develop, produce and deliver products in shorter time than their competitors may acquire higher prices and higher growth.

4.3 HOW TO USE RPT?

4.3.1 Phases of a Product Development Process

There are many possibilities to describe a set of steps or phases which altogether make a product development process. We emphasise on the 'set' because only a complete set guarantees the outcome of a complete product (i.e. regarding function and quality). Of course the sequence of all steps (i.e. their logic and degree of parallelism) influences dramatically the costs and duration of the development process. With regard to classes of prototypes we have to look only at the set of steps. However, if the use and benefit of prototypes are studied, the organisational and management aspects of the development process have to be taken into account as well.

4.3 HOW TO USE RPT?

Although there are many possibilities, the major question is the right description of a product development process. According to VDI 2222 [VDI], which is a German technical guideline, four main phases can be identified:

STEP 1: Idea, market, analysis and planning

It is to become aware of the market needs by help of market analysis, review of research results, customer interviews, patent investigation, etc. As a result of this phase the goal (i.e. product) of the development process has to be defined.

STEP 2: Concept design of product and processes

It is to detail the task and the requirements. Afterwards you have to search for solutions to fulfil the individual functions of the product. Sketches and schemes help to express different ideas. An evaluation of technical and economical aspects provides the best different ideas. An evaluation of technical and economical aspects provides the best combination of functional principles at the end.

STEP 3: Drafting

Now details can be drawn and again an evaluation helps to find out failures which could influence the quality of the product or the manufacturing process.

STEP 4: Design

In this phase final design including simulation and optimisation is done. All information necessary for the further manufacturing process will also be prepared. Afterwards pilot production can start.

Every phase deals with a comprehensive set of requirements, which arise from a life-cycle perspective for the product according to ISO 9004-1 [ISO]. In every phase prototypes can or should be applied to an adequate degree to reach the targeted quality of the product and the targeted costs and time of the development and manufacturing process as well.

4.3.1.1 Development economy

In a development project there is a legal coherence between the costs that are available and the costs which have been used, i.e. they do not occur at the same time. Costs are predisposed in the early stages and especially production related costs can be determined already in the design stage with up to 70%! (Figure 4.5)

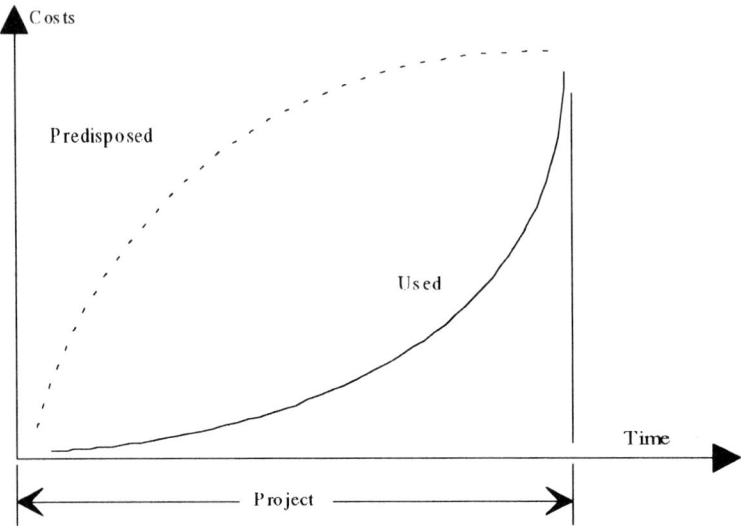

Figure 4.5. Costs are Predisposed in the Early Stages.

This means that the designer should be able to foresee the consequences of his decisions and optimise from a complicated economy model which includes function, production and partly sales. Apart from the early predisposition of the economy there is also a predisposition of the production methods which can be used.

In this connection, a rapid model manufacturing is decisive for the designer. In situations where one would traditionally avoid to make a model due to the immense time consumption, Rapid Prototyping makes it possible to make a model relatively fast. This prompts the designer to make use of physical models more often rather than solely base his decisions on drawing documentation and calculations.

Questions concerning design details and production methods etc can thus be solved more precisely. Correspondingly, possible design errors will be recorded at an early stage of the course of development.

A natural consequence of the iterative product refinement process is that the later in the development process an error is made the more it is related to correction costs. The significance of a rapid error detection is thus extremely important to the economy. (See Figure 4.6)

4.3 HOW TO USE RPT? 53

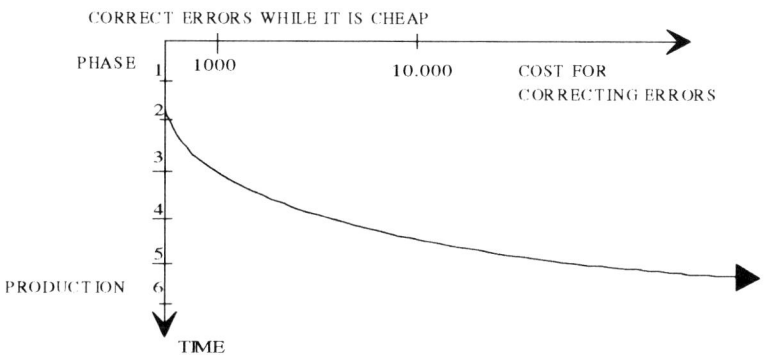

Figure 4.6. Costs for Correcting Errors Related to Time.

4.3.1.2 The Development Process

Once the product concept and type of product have been determined, a series of choices as regards the continuous development of the product will soon arise. Product development is based on compromises amongst alternatives. During the entire course it is therefore necessary to make evaluations and comparisons in order to be able to chose the best solutions to a given situation.

To make a competent choice the designer often uses physical models whereby an actual problem is enlightened. As design to a great extent is a creatively determined activity it is important that the designer can obtain a physical concretised model fast from which he can make his evaluations. The queues in the model shop are therefore fatal for the creativity!

When using conventional model manufacturing techniques, the designer is typically forced to wait for the model for several weeks. The part of the development activities which he tries to illustrate must therefore be put away until the model is available. With the model in his hand the designer is at last able to go on with the problem or - if necessary - ask for another modelling. (Figure 4.7)

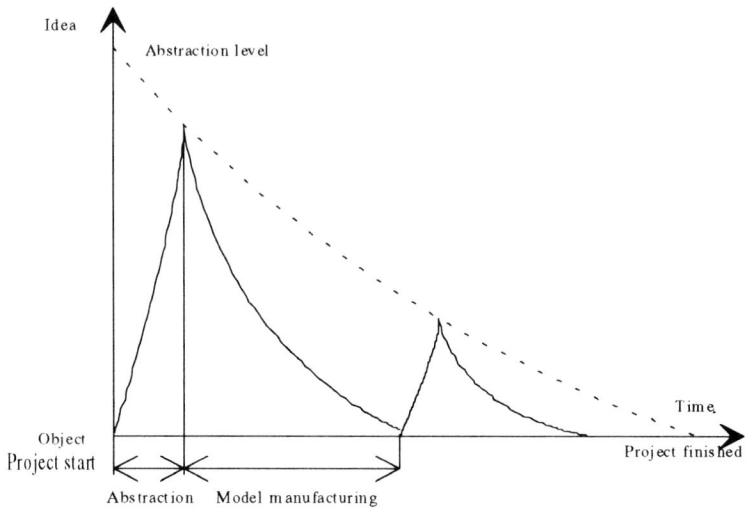

Figure 4.7. Development Course with Traditional Model Manufacturing.

In some cases it can be relevant to question the relevance of the modelled problems once the model is available. It is then possible that the remaining development is already one step further and the modelled problems is thus made unnecessary.

When using Rapid Prototyping, the designer avoids this delay as a model - at best - can be obtained in the course of a few days.

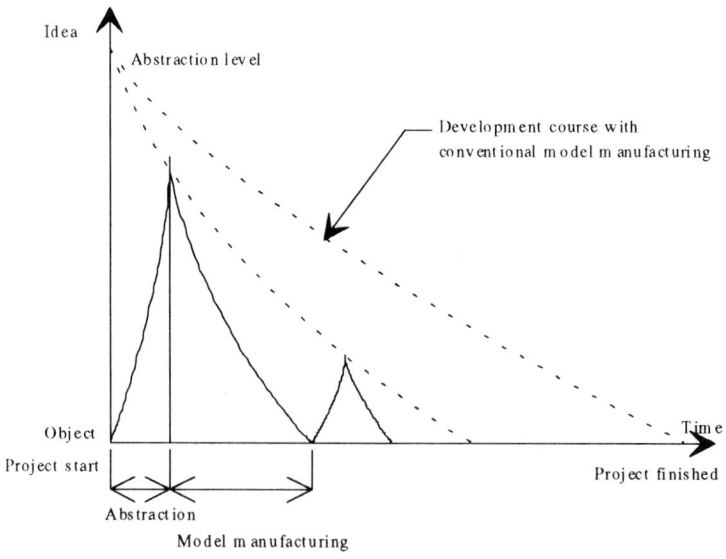

Figure 4.8. Development Course with Rapid Prototyping.

4.3 HOW TO USE RPT?

4.3.2 Models

Models is a concept we all know, feel comfortable with and use daily. If we seek a unambiguous definition to the concept it is, nevertheless, more difficult to understand and a consequent use of the term is difficult to find.

For instance you often hear people mention a new version of a car as the "latest model". As a model is actually a copy of an already existing thing, it may be discussed whether this phrase is just.

In this chapter we seek to uncover the model concept through examples and exposition of various types of models. Finally model descriptions used in this work are described.

4.3.2.1 The model conception

The most appropriate description of the model conception is acquired by comparison to children's play. As children we have all played "grown-ups", i.e. modelled the "world of grown-ups". With simple tools many "daily" situations are recreated and to an outsider (read: grown-up) it can be difficult to see what the play is imitating. This is mainly caused by one thing - the magic touch which makes everything real is missing - fantasy.

Children's age often reflects their level of conscience about their surroundings and their ability to reproduce them. Luckily, there are also some "grown-up" children who have kept this ability. When grown-ups play (model railways, tin soldiers, etc) it is called a hobby.

Figure 4.9. When Children Models Reality.

A good example of children's models is a drawing made by a child. Anybody is able to immediately understand that above drawing is a house under a sky with clouds surrounded by a road and a tree. But what makes us interpret this drawing correctly? This can be related to two important conditions. Firstly we know the background of the sender (child, five years of age, grown up in the western world). Secondly, as receivers we have a pre-knowledge of the item which is modelled (same culture). If there is a disagreement between the two basal conditions the possibility of misinterpretations are numerous.

A model is always a model of "something" (for instance an item or a system). This "something" can be called an object. A model has some properties in common with the object. (See Figure 4.10).

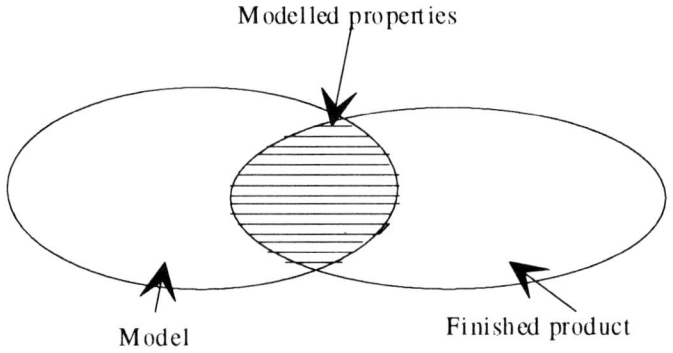

Figure 4.10. Modelled Properties.

A model only contains some of the properties of the object and therefore it deviates from the object. If we once again turn to the child's drawing it is obvious that the modelled properties of the house is a door, two windows with curtains, a roof with a chimney. On the other hand the drawing says nothing about for instance the dimensions of the house or the materials of which it is built.

Some properties of models are quantitative, e.g. weight, dimensions and functions. These can be measured directly and objectively. Others, such as reliability, life-time, assembly friendliness etc, it can be more difficult to measure directly. Properties such as appearance and user-friendliness are not quantitative. They can only be measures subjectively.

4.3.3 Models in Product Development

As known product development is the process a product goes through from the idea is described until the product has been approved for manufacturing. During this process various models are used to a great extent at different abstraction levels.

4.3 HOW TO USE RPT? 57

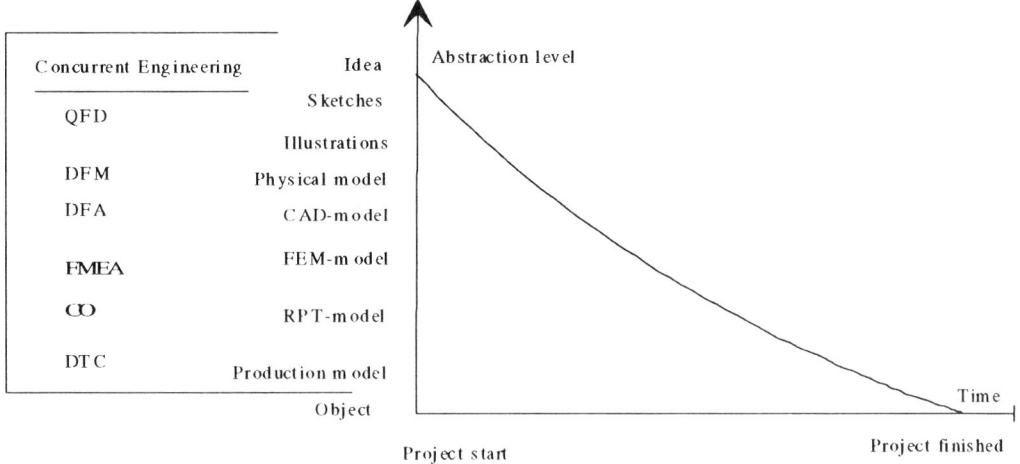

Figure 4.11. Examples of Models Connected to Various Abstraction Levels in Production Development.

Initial Stages - step 1

During the early development stages all decisions and choices are made on incomplete information. At this level, models must therefore be least concrete as you work with loosely formulated concepts and ideas. As the project proceeds, the ideas will be modelled tentatively by means of various techniques corresponding to the stage you are in and the information you seek.

Last Stages - step 2 and 3

Towards the end of the development the models will become more concrete as you approach the finished product. The development is thus a reproduction from model to model and the developer uses a wide range of various product reproduction methods. The modelling can be seen as a way to buy information from the final product and thus reduce the risk to make mistakes. The models vary according to the properties they procure, degree of abstraction, number of details, etc.

Development Tool

Modelling is an important development tool as it allows the participant to describe, visualise, and sculpture his thoughts for the benefit of both himself and others. Gradually, it is generally known and accepted that, to a high degree, the success of a development process depends on the participants' abilities to communicate and visualise their ideas to the other participants of the project group.

In order to use models rationally, a thorough understanding of the modelled properties and the purpose of these is required. The biggest problem is to chose the correct type of model which procure exactly the necessary properties to the actual level of design. If a model includes too many modelled properties at a too early design level, the result will be that too much time, money and energy are spent to product the model. On the other hand it is possible to make the wrong decisions if you try to evaluate more properties than those originally intended for the model.

4.3.3.1 Communication

A model is used for communication - either for communication with others or communication with one self. That which is communicated through the model is information about some of the propertied of the model (see Figure 4.12).

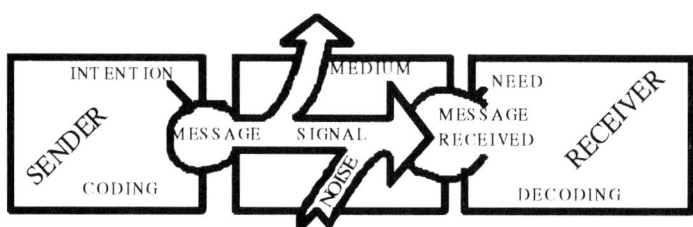

Figure 4.12. The Communication Conception.

In a communication, information is given from a sender to a receiver. The information will be transformed to a signal via a code; the coded signal is a model of the information. The receiver de-codes the signal and only now the receiver has received the information. The code, which for instance can be words, electrical signals. or symbols must therefore be known by both the sender and receiver in order for the information to be transmitted.

The information which the receiver gets can deviate from the information which was sent because the receiver do not understand all signals, the de-coding is wrong or the signal does not come from the sender (noise).

Receiver

When you have to produce a model it is necessary to know who will be using it. Only when the "receiver" is known it can be decided which codes can be used and the technique with which the model shall be made.

In other words: The receiver creates the criteria from which the model can be evaluated. If the receiver understands the codes and if the model can be interpreted clearly in the situation in which it is used, the model fulfils its purpose.

Primarily one has to distinguish between two categories of receivers, namely

4.3 HOW TO USE RPT? 59

"One self"
When communicating with one self during the completion of a product, the model is used in a rather specific way.
In the creative work of the engineer where he gets the ideas which must be formulated, concretised, examined and evaluated, the model acts as a very important supplement to the brains. By means of a model you can partly extend your ability to imagine considerably and partly, the actual manufacturing process demands a thinking process as it is impossible to imagine everything beforehand. The model work therefore reveals uncertainties and this creates questions which again is the occasion of new ideas. The creative work is intensified through this form of self-communication.

"Designer"
Here we understand a designer who receives, either as a colleague with whom you can discuss your problem or another designer who shall take care of part of the project. In both cases it is true that you can communicate thus communication and models supplement each other.

"Management/Technically skilled"
It is true for this group of receivers that a given amount of information shall be transferred in a relatively short time. Furthermore, the project or the ideas must be "sold" to the receivers. This make great demands to the applied models.

"Marketing"
Marketing often uses models to communicate with the public through advertisements and articles and this must be considered a one-way communication without mollification conditions in the form of explaining, accompanying speech. Demands to the finish of the models are big as it must show the final product.

"Workshop/Production Preparation"
When the designer communicates with the workshop it is with the purpose to produce a tool, production equipment or object. This information, which is necessary, must be given clearly and very precisely. Therefore standardised types of drawings, namely construction drawings and assembly drawings, are used. It is, however, more and more common to enclose a physical model with the drawing documentation, as this reduces the risk of errors in the communication and the type of design is understood faster.

4.3.3.2 Superior product development models

In reality, the Concurrent Engineering concept is a superior ideal model for product development supported by a series of models in the form of QFD, DFM, DFA, FMEA, DTC, CO, etc. It is without the frames of this project to enter into a more detailed exposition of these models. It must, however, be mentioned that also here, as with other modelling it is just to question the accordance between the modelled properties and the information which is sought. If we, for instance, look closed at the most used CE-tool QFD (Quality Function Deployment) we see the importance of this accordance. To what extent is it, for instance, possible to predefine the wanted product properties and demands from interested parties in the initial QDF phase, related to the stage in the project you are? The consequence of disagreement between model and reality can, at its best, make the work difficult.

4.3.3.3 Product models

The development process is carried out by applying a series of auxiliaries, the type of which depend on the wanted product and the stage of the development process in which the designer is. Common for all of them is that they were made before a production model could be made and they are produced with emphasis to flexibility as their exquisite purpose is to help the designer with idea generation and evaluation.

The abstraction level of models related directly to the product varies a lot. This does not change the fact that it is fundamental to take a close decision to the degree of details of the modelled properties. The importance of this is reflected clearly when watching a Finite elements Methods (FEM) based strength Calculation of a sheet with a hole exposed to tension. If the designer does not chose the areas closely in which he seeks information, there is both a big risk of misdimensioning the sheet and a far too big calculation time.

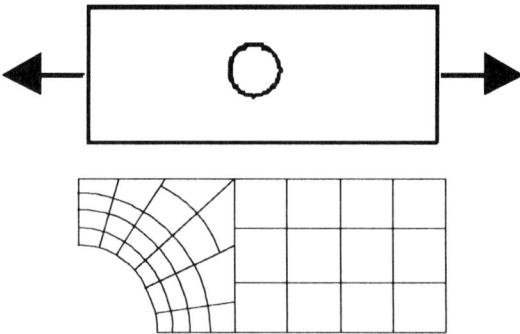

Figure 4.13. Sheet Exposed to Pulling and the Corresponding FEM Element Separation.

4.3 HOW TO USE RPT? 61

The degree of details of the division into elements should finer around the hole in the sheet as this will give a slot effect. As a consequence the biggest tensions will occur here. A too rough division into elements will "blur" this dispersion of tension. The optimum modelling is only acquired by the designer when starting a physical stress test. The possibilities of a designer is here far better than those of for instance a programme developer who must solely depend on paper and the computer monitor in his modelling. Depending on the type of product which is being developed, extremely different modelling tools are used.

4.3.3.4 Model designations

In order to acquire a more systematic knowledge about the big selection of modelling tools in the development stages related to the various development disciplines, a model morphology is appropriate. At present, no formal systematisation of models related to product development has been worked out. This could, nevertheless, make possible an exact description of the precise purpose of modelling and the suitable characteristics of the necessary type of model.

In industry it is unconsciously aimed to systemise types of models by using a series of different designations:

- Working models
- Structural models
- Design models
- Ergonomic models
- Geometric models
- Functional models
- Prototypes.

Common to these designations is that their definition is very indistinct. The significance of these model designations and their succession vary according to the traditions of the different companies and the interpretation of individuals of the designation. The result of this is that when talking about this subject it is often implicit and you cannot be certain that two companies understands the model designation in the same way. The confusion is complete when talking in international connections. In the USA for instance, all types of models are called prototypes, which is seen most clearly from the designation *Rapid Prototyping*. In Denmark you distinguish between a model and a prototype.

4.3.3.5 Designations of models in this project

To (hopefully) avoid too much confusion and misunderstandings we use models as well as prototypes. There is no formal determined definition of the words. Likewise models are not separated into categories as for instance visible models/functional as those designations are seldom exhaustive. To the degree to which it is possible, they are, in stead, supplemented with a more precise model description in which the model are designed according to the following characteristics:

- Type of model (for instance mathematical model, physical model, screen picture, drawing)
- Purpose (for instance simulation, verification, training)
- Sender and receiver group (for instance marketing, designers)
- Coding (for instance drawing by hand, solid modelling)
- Modelled properties (for instance function, structure form)
- Media (for instance clay, plaster, plastics, EDB).

4.3.4 Classes of Models and Prototypes

In above sense a prototype is the result of the concept, design and generation of one or more product characteristics which help the design or development team to test them against user requirements.

According to this definition almost everything can be a model and prototype. A classification is therefore recommended [Steg94].

Design models	 1 : 3	Design review under the consideration of optical, esthetical and ergonomical requirements
Geometrical models		Employed for testing accuracy, form and fit of the later series parts. The focus is on geometry and not on material aspects
Functional models	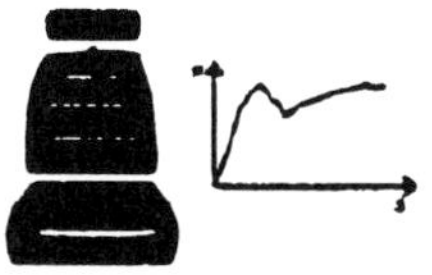	Functional aspects which are represented as a set of features are reviewed (subsystem of a product)
Technical prototypes © IPA / FhG		- All functional aspects of a part but the manufacturing process is different from the one which will be used in the series production - The material may be different from the series part

Figure 4.14. Classification of Models.

4.3 HOW TO USE RPT? 63

As can be seen in Figure 4.3, we have to distinguish the different types of prototypes from pilot production, which we understand as parts where the original manufacturing process will be used for the first time or which consists of the final material whereas the tools are rapidly prototyped.

Design Models
First and foremost these serve as a design review under the consideration of optical, aesthetically and ergonomically requirements, whereas mechanical aspects or accuracy are normally neglected.

Geometrical Models
These are employed for testing accuracy, form and fit of the later series part. Therefore the focus is on geometry and not on material aspects.

Functional Models
These represent a set of features which allow the test of some functional aspects. A functional prototype is usually a subsystem of a product.

Technical Prototypes
These cover all functional aspects of the part and can be used as such. Usually, the manufacturing process is, however, different from the one which will later be used in series production. The technical prototype may also consist of different materials.

Not all prototypes, however, have to be available in a classical sense as physical parts. Let us take a CAD system which allows us to visualise first design drafts or a virtual reality machine which, in the future, is envisaged to become an important design, evaluation and co-operation tool. All these systems provide a non-physical but virtual Prototyping but may comprise all above classes of prototypes.

4.3.4.1 Use of models and prototypes in a development process
The benefit of these prototypes emerges out of their use; four different cases can be identified (see Figure 4.16).

Tool for Communication
Design is a process where a lot of people with different skills and views have to work together on the same product. A member of the top management has to explain his requirements to the designer, a mould maker and an expert for assembly task and vice versa. A prototype acts as a catalyst for such a discussion process.

Expression for Actual Experience

Maybe the customer's requirements are stated clearly at the beginning of a development process. Some uncertainty will, however, exist on how each requirement is fulfilled by a set of individual product features and how they can be put into reality. A prototype is therefore a means of validation and verification and in each stage of the process expresses the consolidated experience of the customer and supplier.

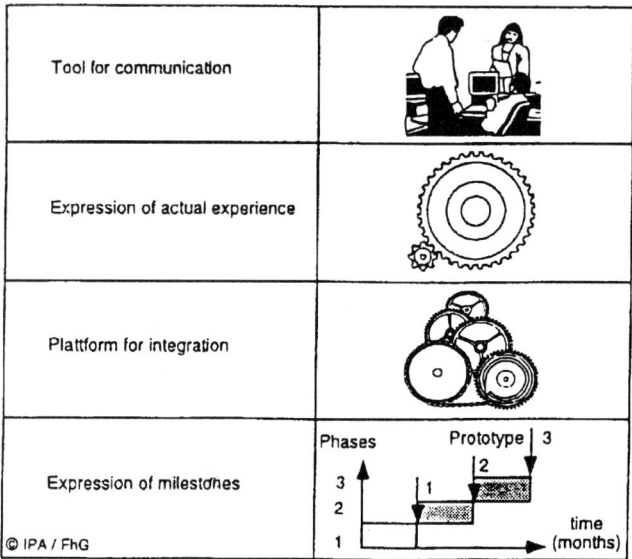

Figure 4.15. Use of Prototypes.

Platform for Integration

As we remember, a functional prototype represents a sub-system of the final product. All sub-systems have to be integrated and tested where constraints of assembly and co-operation have to be considered as vital. Such prototypes are well known as alpha or beta prototypes.

Expression of Milestones

At some stages management and/or the customer normally want to evaluate the progress of the development process. Only in case of a positive evaluation, the project may go on.

4.3.4.2 General benefits of prototypes for a development process

Regarding the classes and the use of prototypes there can be identified against four situations how a prototype can positively influence the development process (see [Ulri94]).

An interesting point is that only in the first case the speed of the prototyping process impacts directly the development process; in all other cases the mere

4.3 HOW TO USE RPT? 65

availability of a prototype (instead of having none) is responsible for a shorter and - due to less iteration cycles - cheaper development.

Acceleration of a Prototyping Process

Prototypes based on RPT or VR techniques can be made more quickly than those made with traditional physical methods (see Figure 4.17). Yet, the benefit depends on the complexity of the prototype and the set of requirements which should be evaluated. Furthermore, there is a large number of prototypes in industry which incorporate electrical or hybrid (both mechanical and electrical) issues. Rapid or virtual prototyping concentrates, however, more on mechanical characteristics (geometry, aesthetics, stress, fatigue, etc) and can - at least within a short-term view - only apply in a phase of the development process which addresses these issues.

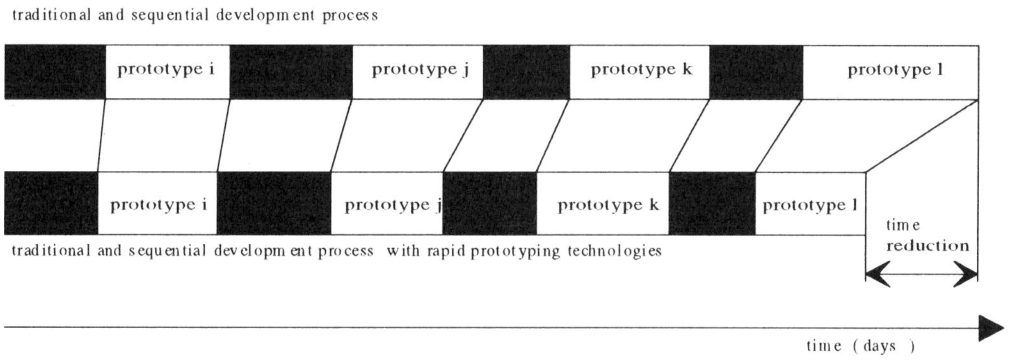

Figure 4.16. Acceleration of the Prototyping Process.

A Prototype Influences later Development Phases:

In this case the prototype acts as a communication tool within the team and improves the decision finding. Tool design can, for instance, be made more quickly if a 3D description of the part - instead of a set of 2D drawings - is available (see Figure 4.17) or a complex physical prototype may no longer be necessary because a computer simulation provides the desired results (e.g. crash behaviour simulation).

Figure 4.17. Influence of a Prototype on Later Phases.

A Prototype Improves the Success Rate of a Development Process:
Especially an early prototype allows a quick verification of the assumption of the product development process. The reliability of this information which serves as input to the next development phase increases and also the probability of cost consuming changes in a later state decreases (see Figure 4.18). The costs of a prototype, however, have to be compared to those of a product change. Prototyping is therefore only recommended for risky and expensive products.

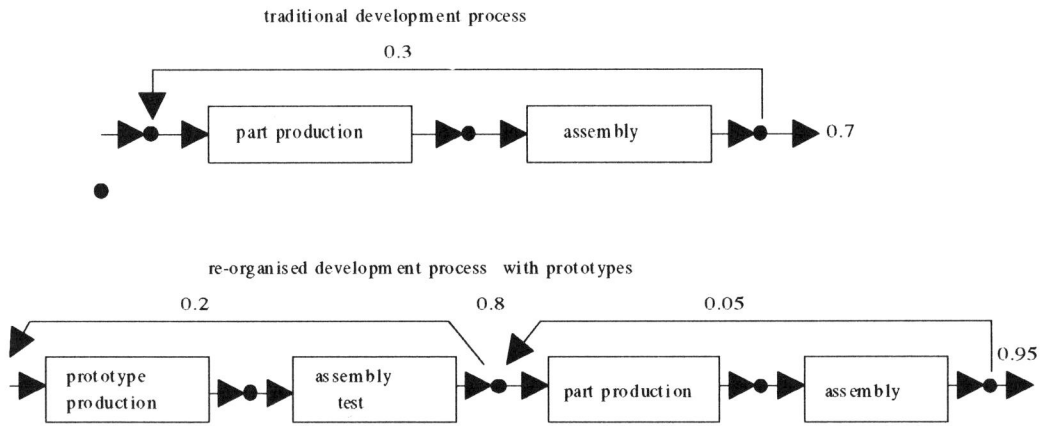

Figure 4.18. Increase of the Success Rate of a Development Process.

4.3 HOW TO USE RPT? 67

A Prototype influences the Sequence of the Development Phases

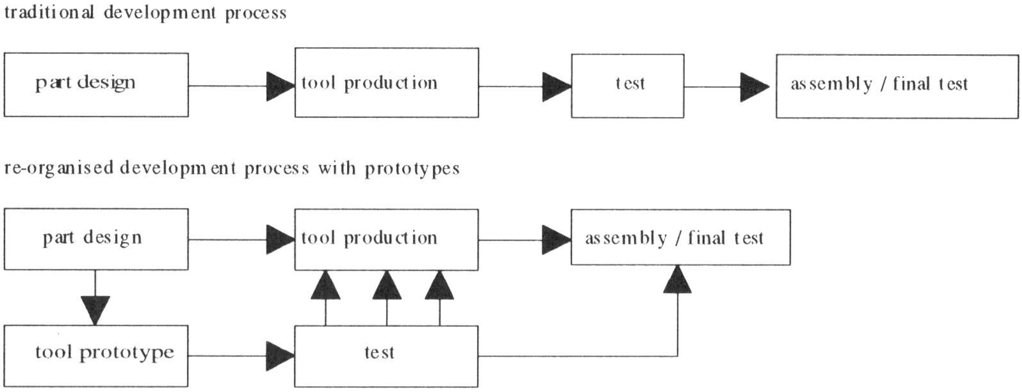

traditional development process

```
part design → tool production → test → assembly / final test
```

re-organised development process with prototypes

```
part design → tool production → assembly / final test
     ↓            ↑ ↑ ↑
tool prototype → test
```

Figure 4.19. Reorganisation of the Development Process by Prototypes.

Figure 4.19 explains the conventional sequence of the design of an injection mould. Tests of the mould can be done only after it has been almost finished. Final assembly and test is influenced in the line by a sequential process. A prototype (physical or virtual) helps to test the tool at an early stage and reduces both development time and uncertainty.

The use of prototypes in a development process reveals some key conclusions:

- The benefit of prototypes comes merely from the fact that we use prototypes without regard to whether they are physical or virtual.
- The organisation of the development process (i.e. which prototype has to be used at which stage) has to be identified therefore as the critical point.
- There is, however, no generic organisation of a development process. It depends on the individual product.
- A flexible, fast, cost and quality effective development process combines a series of prototyping technologies. Virtual methods (CAD, simulation, FEM, VR, etc) should both be applied dependent on the specific tasks in the process.

4.3.4.3 From models to tools

Up to now, Rapid Prototype technologies have evolved relatively independently from most other processes of fabrication. This was normal since this just born branch of production technologies mostly aimed to answer to requests concerning the first three types of industrial prototypes:

- Aesthetic Models (= Design Models)
- Geometrical Models
- Functional Prototypes

Nowadays, state of the art has promoted many of these infant technologies to a sufficient degree of maturity for performances that fulfil most of the needs of these Prototypes.

Actually, physical properties and geometrical qualities are so good that a new area of application of these techniques is taking shape and could even be supplanting in importance the former one:

Fabrication of Technological Prototypes and necessarily Prototype Tools.

Technological Prototypes are in many manufacturing areas a compulsory development phase, plastic injection moulding being one of the most demanding techniques in this regard.

RPT is able to provide directly or indirectly in combination with what is called *Post RPT Technologies* manufacturing tools, likely to produce from 1 to 10.000 parts, "just like" the production item.

Main production methodologies emendable to these developments are presented, with their general characteristics.

Direct Tooling

This means that independently of any other technology, RPT provides a tool which is usable in a conventional production process.

There is actually only one such technology, still in the BETA phase: Soligen's DSCP (Direct Shell Production Casting). With this LMT technique, based on a MIT development, a ceramic shell is produced by controlled distribution of adhesives on ceramic powder. The shell may directly be used as such in the lost wax process, offering a very interesting access to rapid production of metallic parts, or even metallic tools.

Other RPT are used to provide directly cavities or cores for different processing techniques, but most of them are still in the R&D phases.

Indirect Tooling

A very large number of Post RPT technologies allow in some way or another to produce technological prototypes. Most of them are still in the R&D phase, but be sure that some will mature as an efficient way to get much more than a prototype tool.

4.3 HOW TO USE RPT?

4.3.4.4 Related product development tools and methods

A large number of tools and methods have been developed to support the different functions engaged in the product development. Here only a few are mentioned and only a short summary of each is given.

Design for Manufacture and Assembly

Assesses design variations for their ease of assembly, provides pointers on where design can be improved. Helps engineers to make better decisions during the early stages and reduces costs.

Design to Cost

Aims at monitoring and controlling costs to a fixed target during the product introduction process. Companies use Design to Cost at early stages of product development.

Failures Modes & Effect Analysis (FMEA)

Dedicated for the quality improvement of product and process design. It identifies potential failures which could occur during design, manufacturing and working life of products, components and processes. It indicates opportunities to improve the design thorough preservative action, having identified the potential failures, causes and allocated priorities. It aims at getting right the first time.

Quality Function Deployment

A method for identifying at early stages of the production process which parameters are the most critical in satisfying the customers' needs and the priories requirements for design and production.

Taguchi Method

Methodology to provide robust design and processes and a structural approach to product and process design, and a customer oriented definition of quality.

Application Type of model		Model Properties	Product Development	Foundation for Decision — Production preparation	Foundation for Decision — Tool Production	Foundation for Decision — Sub-supplier
3D CAD model Virtual model Virtual prototype		Screen picture with a total description of geometry. Coloured paper copy of screen picture	Evaluate - Design - Disclose errors - Simulate, calculate	- Evaluation - Communication - Simulation, animation	Evaluation Communication	Evaluation Communication
Design Model	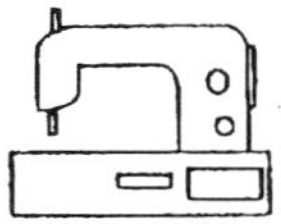	Good surfaces and correct external geometry	Design Ergonomy Market test	Initiate choice of technology	Evaluation Communication	Evaluation Communication
Geometry Model	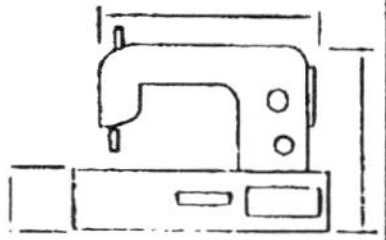	Exact geometrical measures	Follow-up - Disclose errors - Test/confirm design	Evaluate - Choice of process - Assembly - Quality control	Evaluate - Tool production principles	Involve sub-supplier Collect quotation - Tools - Special equipment
Functional Model	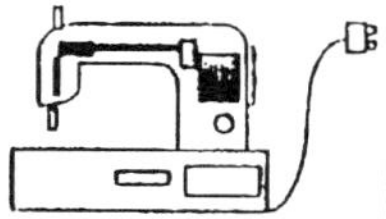	Approximate material	After test - Functions - Principles - Optimization	Follow-up Tools Methods	Tool production Make or buy	Follow-up at sub-supplier
Prototype	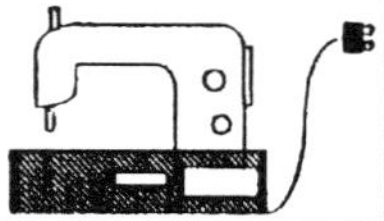	Correct material and approximate process	Test - Standard - Customer demands	Produce - Production tools and fixtures - Test objects	Produce - Production tools and fixtures - Test objects	
0-series	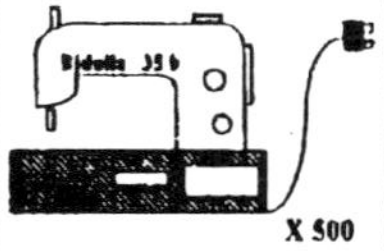	Final material Final process	Test Introduction to market	Test production and commissioning		

Figure 4.20. Main Product Methologies.

5 LMT IN CASTING

5.1 INTRODUCTION

FFF (Free Form Fabrication) is a technique which is developing at a rapid rate. Increased accuracy combined with rapid development of new materials result in accurate and durable models mostly made of different types of polymers.

Unfortunately, the materials used for FFF are not normally used in series production. Photopolymers and paper laminates do not have the same properties as ABS or polyamide. Therefore, it is not possible to make functional tests. For cases where production materials like ABS or nylon are used, the FFF-machine does not use the same process as in series production. The materials can for instance be sintered or extruded into parts, which resultin porous or orthotropic parts and they do not behave as parts made in series production.

In order to obtain a part with correct properties, it must be manufactured

- of correct production material
- by the correct production process

One way to achieve this is to make the tool for the part by FFF. At present two areas attract primary interest from the industry, the manufacture of

- cast metal parts
- injection-moulded plastic parts

The first technique to be used in connection with FFF is casting. During 1995 FFF has been increasingly used both for sand casting and lost wax casting. The prototypes made are mostly for cases where the demand for short leadtimes is important.

The methods for making tools for injection-moulded plastic parts are under development. In Germany a company called EOS has developed a machine for sintering metal tools directly. Other manufacturers are working on different processes for making sintered metal parts. Experiments have been made by using tool cavities from photo polymers. If these materials can be made to withstand higher temperatures and with better heat conductivity they will represent an alternative.

There are several ways of using FFF as a tool for making castings, but the three main principles are:

1. Casting patterns directly made by the FFF method. According to this principle a model is made for each casting. The procedure is mostly used for lost wax casting. The FFF model is burned out and destroyed. This makes the method more suitable for just one or a few parts. There are several FFF processes well suited for this principle. Stratasys can make parts directly of wax. LOM and SLS parts are often used as patterns. The latest quick cast method for the SLA process also seams to work well.
2. Casting moulds directly made by the FFF method. According to this principle the negative geometry (a mould) is made of the part that is to be manufactured. This is contrary to the first principle. Also for this principle there is one mould for each casting. The latest process that uses this principle is EOSINT S from EOS. But also DSPC (Direct Shell Production Casting) from Soligen belongs to this group.
3. Patterns and moulds indirectly made by the FFF method. According to this principle the tools to be used in the foundary process are made by the FFF method. Thus it is possible to make several articles at a time. Some examples are patterns and core boxes for sand casting, tools to make wax patterns for the lost wax process, tools for plaster casting or core boxes for die casting. All FFF processes can be used to indirectly make tools. A substantial amount of CAD-work is often required to make patterns for sand casting, core boxes or other foundary tools. This adds to the lead time for casting. Using silicon castings is one way of avoiding time-consuming operations.

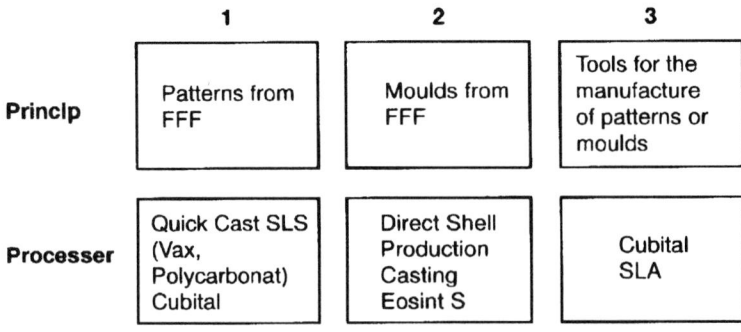

Figure 5.1. Principles for Using FFF for Castings.

5.1 INTRODUCTION

It is important to choose the most suitable method or principle for the purpose. Factors that should affect the choice are:

- *Lead time*. If the lead time is critical, the quickest method must be chosen
- *Number of parts*. Each FFF detail is expensive. If a large number of parts is to be manufactured, it is cheaper to make tools that can be used to make many castings
- *Size of part*. Some processes become expensive, if the size of the part is large
- *Complexity of part*. For more complex geometry lost wax casting is more suited. Simpler details can be made at a lower cost if moulds or patterns are made instead.

5.2 SAND CASTING

During the last six months of 1995 the demand for sand casting tools manufactured by the FFF method increased significantly. One reason is that many companies have introduced solid modelling CAD systems, which makes it easy to create the files necessary for making FFF models. Another reason is that many companies want 5 - 20 prototypes in metal as soon as possible after completion of the design work. The geometry is often checked in the actual manufacture of the FFF part. By making the part with shrinkage compensation a "free" attern for sand casting is obtained and a casting can be ordered the same day as the design has been approved.

Sand casting is a frequently used casting method. The size of the foundries varies from small family companies, where each casting is made by hand to large volume foundries, where the process is fully automated. Also the size of the casting varies. FFF is often used to make short series or prototypes. A short lead time is often the most important factor. It is recommendable to find out, what types of products the foundry generally makes and what types of alloys that are normally used. Small foundries, which are used to cast prototypes, are often best suited.

5.2.1 The Sand Casting Process

The typical flow of work in the design of the tools used for making a sand casting is described below. A pattern is used for sand castings. The pattern describes the geometry of the casting. To compensate for the metal shrinkage that occurs during the solidification of he metal, the model is made larger than the part,

1 % larger for aluminum and 1.8 % for steel. The scaling should be performed in the FFF machine, as late as possible in the development process, to avoid mistakes.

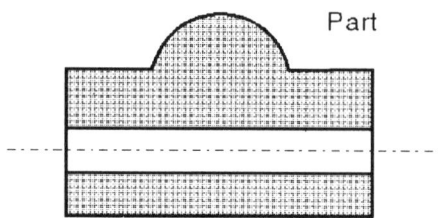

Figure 5.2. The Part to Be Cast.

In order to make it possible to form two mould parts of sand the model has to be divided into two halves. The line (more exactly a surface or a plane) that divides the model into two halves is called a parting line or parting plane. The two model halves are mounted on pattern plates. The models must be placed exactly opposite each other on the pattern plates to avoid dislocation of the casting.

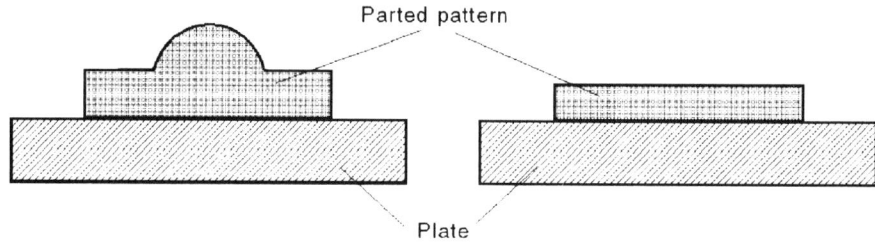

Figure 5.3. The Models on the Pattern Plate.

Drafts should be added to enable an easy removal of the model halves from the mould. The geometry for the core prints have to be added as well.

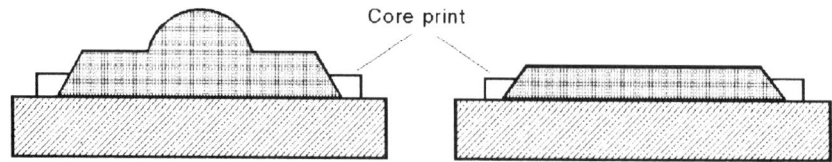

Figure 5.4. The Models with Drafts and Core Print Geometry.

To avoid that the core sticks and to prevent it from falling to the bottom, it should be made with a smaller diameter than the core print. A gap of between 0.1

5.2 SAND CASTING

and 0.4 mm is feasible. For circular coreprints the last portion up to the split line should be a chamfer to avoid zero draft angles. The chamfer should have an angle of 6-10 degrees.

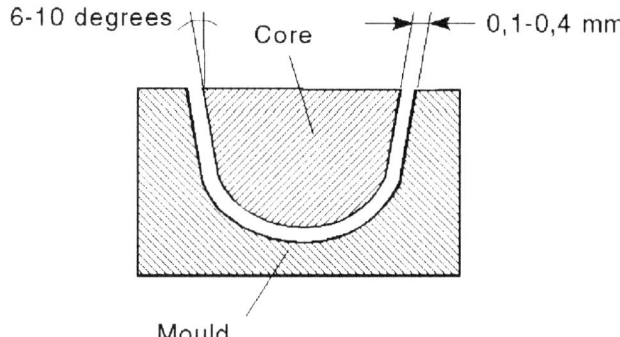

Figure 5.5. To Let the Core Fall Down in the Coreprint it Must Be Correctly Designed.

Finally the cores must be made in core boxes. The cores have ends, which will fit into the core prints. If the core geometry has been created separately in the CAD system, it is easy to design the core boxes. In those cases where the split line is flat, the core geometry can be subtracted from two blocks and the result is the core box. For some complicated parts many core boxes are necessary.

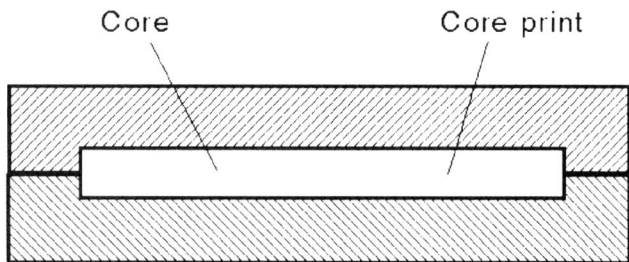

Figure 5.6. The Corebox.

Sand is then poured on the models to create an inprint in the sand. The cores are placed in the mould and the two mould halves are closed. The melted metal is

76   5 LMT IN CASTING

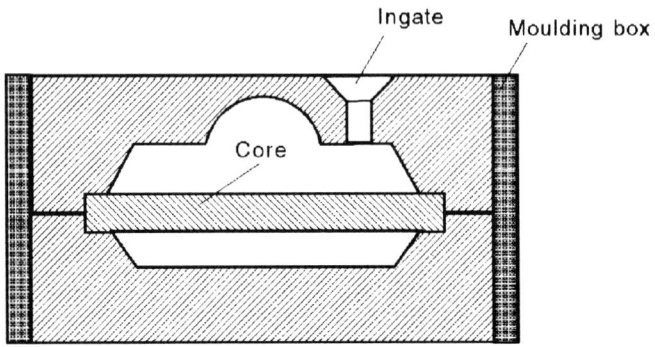

Figure 5.7. The Mould Ready for Pouring.

5.2.2 Different Ways of Combining FFF With Sand Casting

There are in principle three different ways of using FFF for manufacturing sand casting tools.

- Tool design in a CAD system
- Direct use of FFF models
- Indirect use of FFF-models

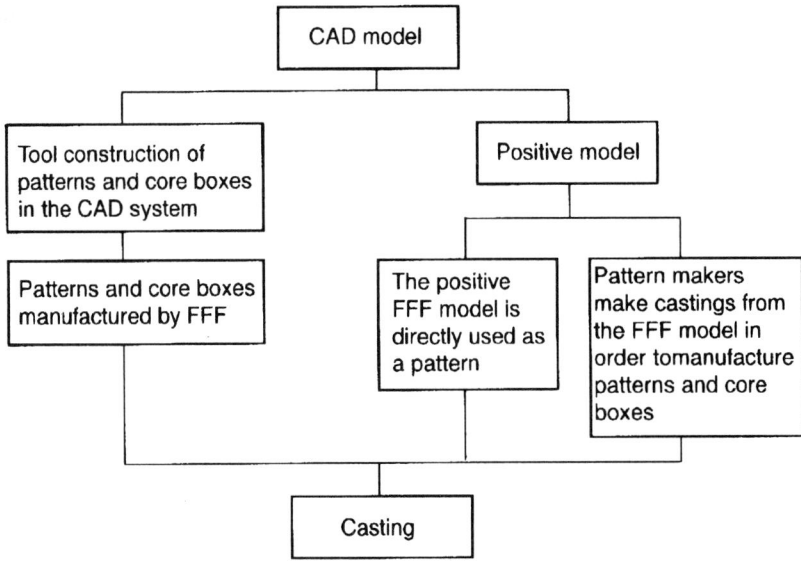

Figure 5.8. The Principles for Combining FFF With Sand Casting.

5.2 SAND CASTING

5.2.2.1 Tool design in a CAD system

Normally the final part is designed in the CAD system. Cast parts must have machining tolerances added. From this part a pattern is created. Some CAD programmes contain special modules which makes the design of tools easier.

By designing the tools in the CAD system the engineer can make sure that the design is also easy to produce. The effort put into designing tools can also be of value in making series production tools.

A disadvantage is, however, that the process is time-consuming. Radii and draft angles can take a long time to design. During the concept phase one would often like to minimize the time for creating details, since the concept of the whole design might change after the first test. But since sand castings require draft angles they have to be added to the CAD model. If one wants to avoid adding draft angles, the lost wax method can be an alternative in some cases.

5.2.2.2 Direct use of FFF models

The quickest way to manufacture a casting is to use a model, that has been directly compensated for shrinkage, in the casting process. This is possible for simple geometries. Complicated split planes can also be created in the sand by forming the sand manually by following the steps below.

1. The model is placed in the lower part of the mould and sand is shaped by hand to create a split line.
2. The upper part of the mould is placed on top of the lower and sand is poured into the mould. The upper mould is removed and replaced with a new one. The process is repeated to create enough upper moulds.
3. The last upper mould is left on the lower mould. The two moulds are then turned upside down. The lower part of the mould is now on top.
4. Step 2 is repeated for the lower mould.

A full set of upper and lower moulds are now created. The only thing left to do is to create the gating and to cast the parts.

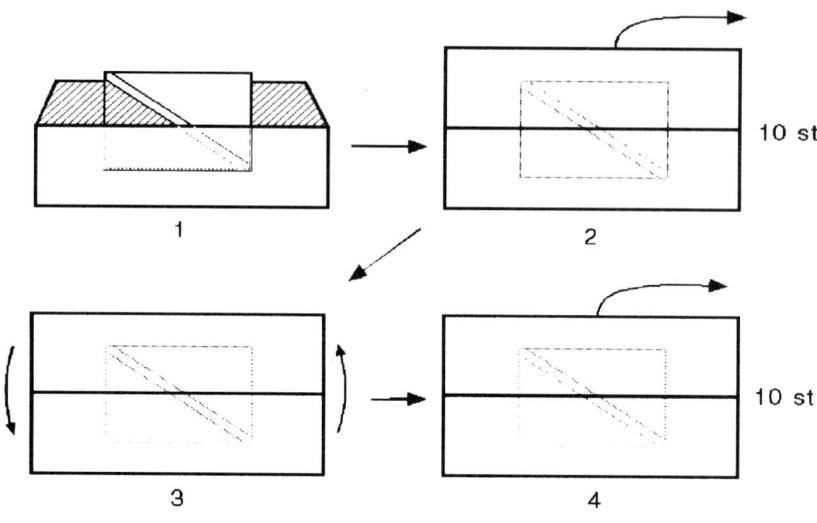

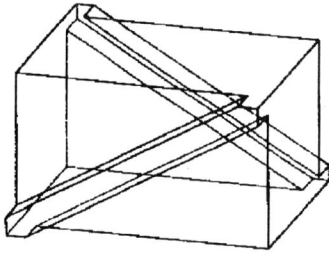

Figure 5.9. How to Make Castings Directly From an FFF Model.

5.2.2.3 Indirect use of FFF models

According to the third method a positive FFF model is used to create the sand casting tools. This is done in several steps. In the first step a positive shrinkage-compensated model is made. The tools are then made by making reproductions twice, from positive to negative and back again, in silicon and plastic. The split lines are created during the reproduction. Generally this work would be done in the CAD system as is described earlier. Since the pattern maker does this work by hand the engineer does not have to spend time creating the tool in the CAD system. On the other hand it also means that the accuracy of the casting decreases. Normally a pattern maker has to do the reproductions. It is rarely done by the foundry. This adds a step to the process.

5.3 PLASTER CASTING

The process for making castings of plaster is similar to the sand casting process. The main difference is that plaster or gypsum is used instead of sand. The patterns can be made of wood, aluminum, plastic or silicon rubber. The advantage of rubber is that small undercuts can be made. The plaster gives a high surface quality and the surface finish is similar to that obtained when making die castings. If FFF tools are used directly, they have to be polished to a high surface finish to avoid that the tools stick to the plaster. Plaster castings can be used for metals with low melting points like aluminum and magnesium. It is not possible to cast ferro metals in plaster.

5.4 LOST WAX AND LOST FFF CASTING

The lost wax process can easily be combined with FFF. There are two lost wax foundries in the Nordic countries, TPC in Sweden and SacoTech in Finland. TPC have been involved in different FFF projects since 1993 and are familiar with the making of castings by FFF using different techniques. The advantage of lost wax castings is that complex and complicated shapes can be cast directly from an FFF model without making any tools. When many castings should be manufactured, the tooling can be made of FFF material strong enough to withstand the wax that is used as the normal pattern material. During 1995 the number of lost wax castings made in combination with different FFF techniques has increased significantly. Mostly prototypes, spare parts and short series are manufactured.

5.4.1 The lost wax process
The basic lost wax process is described below:

- The patterns used are made from wax and by injection moulding. The injection process is similar to the process used in the plastic industry. The tools are often made of aluminum since the wax has a melting point of 70 oC and are non-agressive. The dimensions of the tool have to be compensated for the shrinkage of both wax and metal. A pattern can be built by combining many wax patterns. With this method complex parts can be made with simple tools.
- The wax patterns are mounted on a wax tree. Thus many parts can be made in the same mould. It is important that the tree is correctly made so that the melted metal can be fed into the mould without creating defects or sinkings in the casting.

- The wax tree is dipped into a ceramic slurry. Then sand is poured over the wet surface to strengthen the shell. The first layer is especially fine to give a high surface finish. The process is repeated with courser sand. The last layers additionally strengthen the shell. The layers have to be porous enough, though, to let the shell breathe.
- The mould is now completed and filled with wax. The wax is removed by blowing hot steam into the mould. The wax melts quickly and flows out of the mould. The quick heating is important to prevent the shell from cracking. The wax has a heat expansion much larger than the ceramic shell. The shell is now almost completed. The last remains of wax is burnt out in the oven process that follows.
- To avoid thermally shocking the shell when it is filled with melted metal, the shell is heated to 1 100 oC before being cast.
- When cooled the shell is cracked and removed. Chemicals are used to clean the channels and cavities when mechanical cleaning is impossible. Chemical cleaning cannot be used on aluminim.

The above described foundry process is a standard process. The advantage of the process is that good accuracy and a high surface finish, which yields fewer machining operations to finish the part, are obtained (see Figure 5.10 below).

5.4.2 Different Methods of Combining FFF With Lost Wax Casting

There are three principles for using FFF as a tool to make castings. For lost wax castings the methods are:

Patterns made by FFF. For each casting that shall be manufactured, an FFF model is made. This FFF model is used instead of a wax pattern. Since the FFF-pattern must be burned out of the ceramic shell, the method becomes expensive for many and large details. Another problem is that the shell can crack during the burn out of the pattern. There is also a risk for remaining ashes and dust after the burn out. TPC have therefore developed methods that make it possible to produce high quality castings with short lead times.

Moulds made by FFF. By manufacturing the moulds directly using FFF methods, single castings can be made quickly. At present there are two processes using this principle. The latest machine in use is the EOSINT S from EOS. The machine comes in two different sizes. These machines work according to a process similar to the SLS process; powder is sintered with a laser layer by layer. The layers are 0.2 mm thick and the material is a type of foundry sand. It is possible to make the mould in either one piece or several pieces. When the mould is manufactured the excess sand is poured out of the mould. Cores and runners can be manufactured as an integrated part of the mould. The process is, therefore,

5.4 LOST WAX AND LOST FFF CASTING

more similar to the lost wax process than to the sand casting process. Since the mould is always larger than the part, the block becomes relatively large, which ought to result in relatively long manufacturing times.

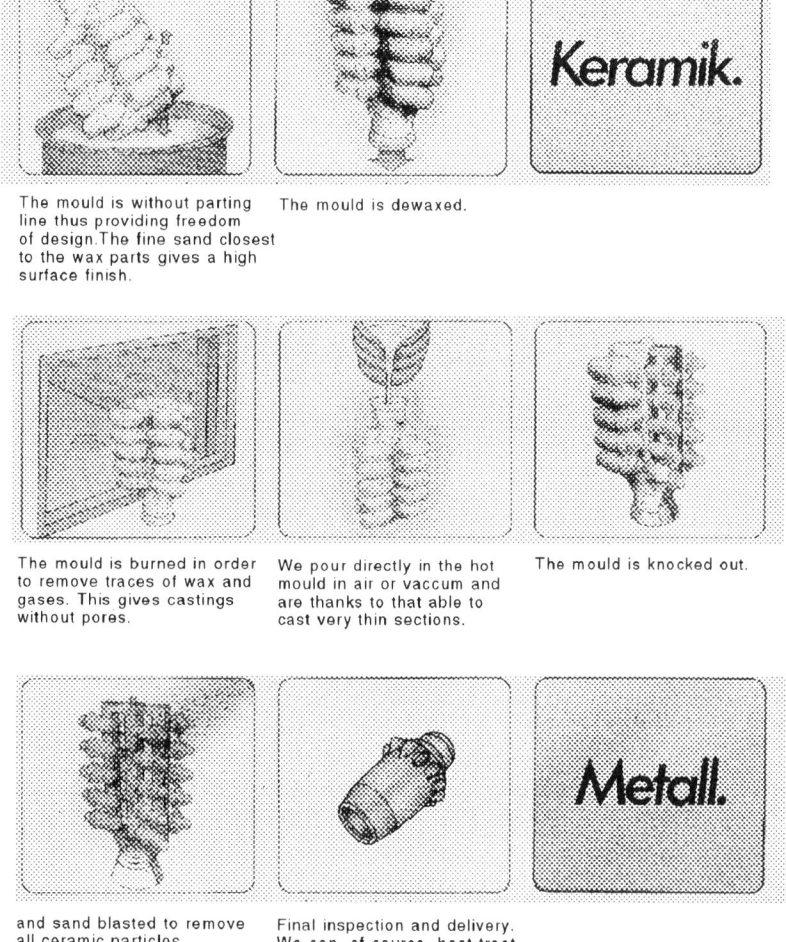

Figure 5.10. The Lost Wax Process.

The other process is "Direct Shell Production Casting" (DSCP) and the equipment is manufactured by Soligen with a licence from MIT. The company has been developing the equipment for a relatively long period of time, but has only sold a few machines so far. The DSPC process is similar to the EOS process, with the difference that the material is glued using a technique similar to an ink jet printer. If EOS uses material from the sand casting industry, Soligen have chosen to use material developed for the lost wax industry. The company has also bought a small foundry in order to to sell castings made with short lead times.

Wax tools manufactured directly or indirectly by FFF. The direct method requires that the tool design is created in a CAD system. The material used in many FFF processes can withstand the temperature of melted wax. Therefore the FFF tools can be used directly to create wax patterns. The heat conduction is not as good as that of for example aluminum and this results in longer cooling cycles. The required CAD work is the same as described in the sand casting section. SINTEF have done several projects using this method.

By the indirect method, a silicon mould is made from a positive FFF model. The silicon is flexible and negative drafts can be made. It is also possible to make holes and simple cavities. The wax may not fill the mould completely if the walls of the mould are too thin (less than 6 mm). It may also be a problem to make solid parts. The wax shrinks during the solidification and voids can occur. To avoid this problem the mould can be filled with solid wax before the liquid wax is injected. Using this method relatively many parts can be created to a reasonable cost.

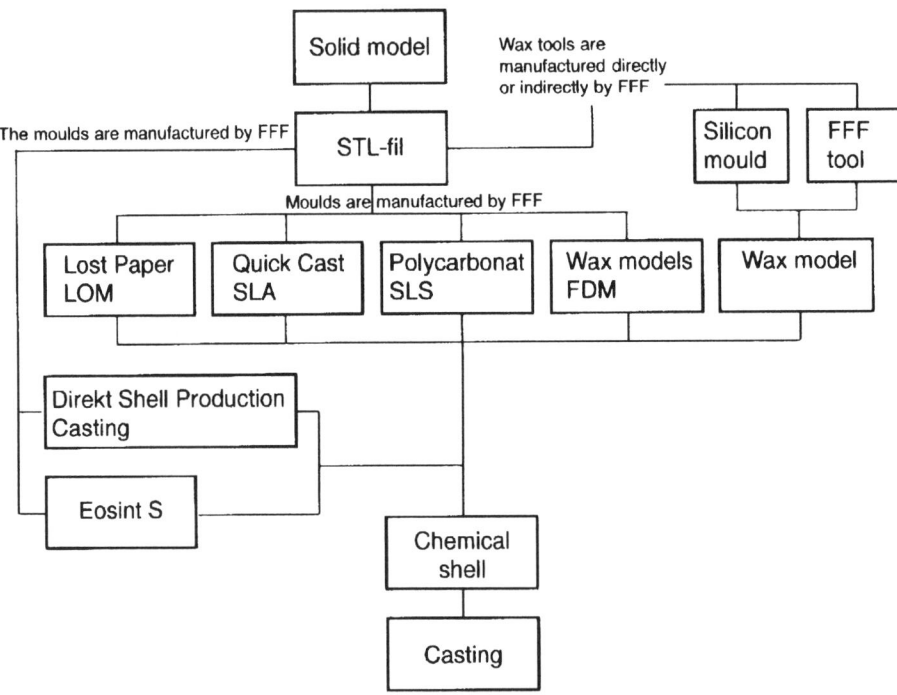

Figure 5.11. Different Methods to Make Castings by Combining FFF and Lost Wax Castings.

5.5 PLASTIC INJECTION MOULDING

This chapter describes the various test and experiments that have been carried out in this project. They are organised after theme, and are not sequential in time.

Most of the tests are performed on site SINTEF, but in some case we needed external assistance to complete the test.

The tests with the synthetic design elements are made in the in-house moulding machine. The mother tool is prepared with a centrally located injection nozzle, and has two cavities for inserts Ø 70 mm, one on each side. The fixed plate insert has a depth of 4 mm, while the movable plate has a depth of 15 mm

5.5.1 Test 1, Synthetic Design Element 1
Purpose
The purpose of this test was simply to demonstrate the feasibility of injecting thermoplastic material in FFF cavities.
Test parameters
- Material: Polystyrene
- Size: Ø 60 mm, height 10 mm, thickness 1 mm
- Temperature:
- Holding pressure:
- Cycle time:

Case history
The product was a conic tray with an imprint "SINTEF" in the bottom. The insert was assembled wit the mother tool, and the surface was coated with a wax based release agent. A colourless polystyrene was injected in the mould.

Results
After 15 shots the gate was broken on one of the inserts. The general quality as expected, but the impression of the surface quality is low compared to a production tool performance. The moulded part repeat the mould surface excellent, and it is easy to see the individual layers from the FFF process. The edge at the parting surface is irregular.

Conclusions
Test is successful, the feasibility is demonstrated.

5.5.2 Test 2, Synthetic Design Element 2
Purpose
The purpose of this test was to check the strength of different geometrical elements. Also different materials were tested.

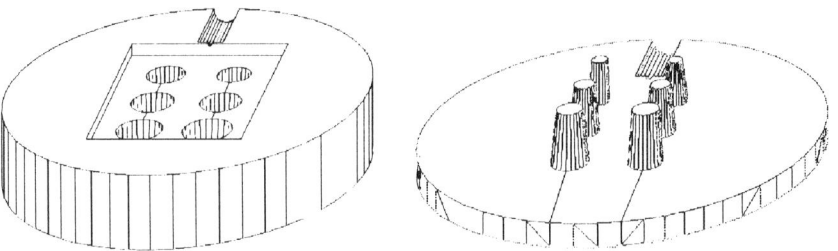

Figure 5.12. LMT Inserts for Test Part 2.

Test parameters
- Material: Polypropylene, Nylon
- Size: Base plate 30 x 40 mm, thickness 2 mm, 6 conic towers with height 6,3 - 8,5 mm, outside diameter 6 - 8 mm (the core towers on the fixed tool plate have diameter 3,3 - 6,5 mm). Draft angles are 2,2° - 6.2°.
- Temperature:
- Holding pressure:
- Cycle time:

Case history

The product was a rectangular plate with 6 hollow conic towers. The tool is shown in figure . The tool was assembled in the mother tool and coated with a wax based release agent. Plastic material was injected into the cavity. After the first mould broke, it was replaced by a second copy, and a new material was tested.

Results

After 5 injections, the thinnest cores broke. The test continued, and 20 parts were made before the gate was destroyed.

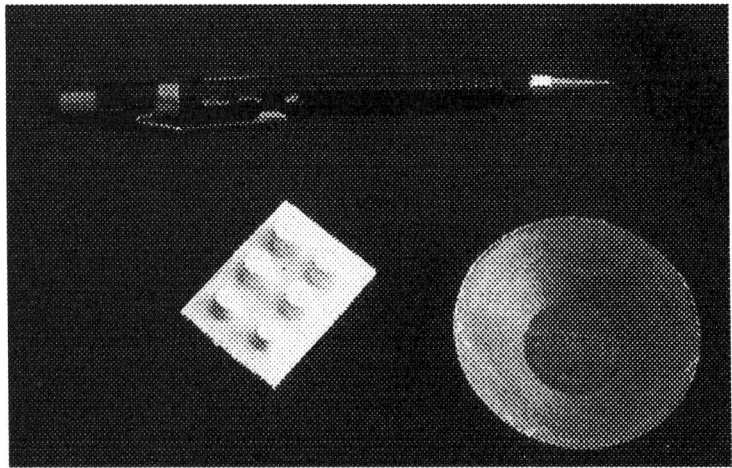

Figure 5.13. Synthetic Design Element 1 (right) and 2 (left).

5.5 PLASTIC INJECTION MOULDING

Conclusions

The thinnest elements could not stand the opening force. The main reason for this is the poor surface finish of the mould. Both the polypropylene and the nylon model were good apart from the broken core.

Dimension stability is very good

5.5.3 Test 3, Extractor for Print Boards
Purpose

The purpose of this test was to demonstrate the feasibility of this method on a real part. A new material was added to the test.

Test parameters
- Material: Acrylnitrilbutadienstyrene (ABS)
- Size: Rectangular 30 x 40 mm, height 8 mm, thickness variable, max. 4 mm
- Temperature:
- Holding pressure:
- Test 3Cycle time:

Case history

The extractor was a difficult part even with silicone rubber casting, which had been tried before. The was a 2 mm overhang at the front side, and holes from both sides. For the mould, the holes were plugged. The fixed part of the mould was split in order to remove the core under the overhang.

To get the part out of the mould, the fixed part was not glued to the mother tool. After injection, the tool was opened, but since the fixed insert was not glued, it followed the part. The insert had to be removed manually.

At a certain stage of the insert design, it was planned to include an ejector to this test. This decision was altered, and the hole for the ejector pin was filled with epoxy.

Results

After the first shot, the epoxy sealing of the ejector hole melted, and the mould was ruined.

Conclusions

ABS functioned as well as injection material as the others tested before.

5.5.4 Test 4, Lamp Brightness Control Wheel
Purpose

Same as for test 3.

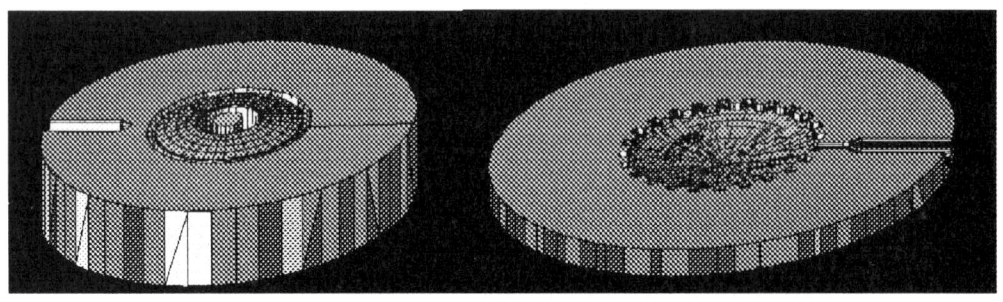
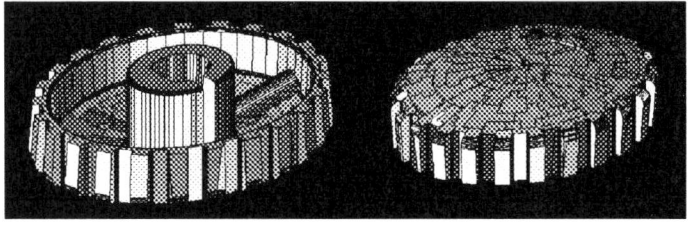

Figure 5.14. LMT Inserts for the Lamp Brightness Control Wheel (top), and the Product Itself (bottom).

Test parameters
- Material: Polyethylene
- Size: Ø 30 mm, height 5,8 mm, thickness 0,9 mm
- Temperature:
- Holding pressure:
- Cycle time:

Case history

This small control wheel was an ideal product for these tests: small and with relative complex details. It was prepared the same way as the other test parts, but two different colours of the test material was applied.

Results

After 3 shot, the internal ring broke. This incident was obviously caused by poor surface finish of the mould. The test continued, and another 20 parts were made.

Some fractions in the parting surface appeared after 10 shots, shell shaped fragments of the mould broke loose.

Conclusions

Adding dark colours makes the details more visible, it was easy to see the layers from the FFF process.

5.5.5 Test 5, Telephone Cover

Purpose

The purpose of this test was to demonstrate the process on a large, real product.

5.5 PLASTIC INJECTION MOULDING

Test parameters
- Material: Polyoxymethylene (POM)
- Size: Rectangular 186 x 140 mm, height 22 mm, thickness 2 mm
- Temperature:
- Holding pressure:
- Cycle time:

Case history

The telephone cover was prepared at SINTEF and brought to an external plastic injection moulding company. Due to the size we needed higher pressure capacity to fill the cavity.

The inserts were not really inserted into a mother tool, they were assembled on a two base plates.

Results

The first shots did not fill the cavity, and the operator increased the fill volume for the next 5 shots. The cycle time was obviously too high, small cracks started to appear around the injection nozzle. These cracks opened during the succeeding shots, and the test was stopped after 15 shots without a completely filled mould.

The last parts made had increased thickness in certain areas, and the cracks in the mould was represented as extra, very thin walls around the nozzle.

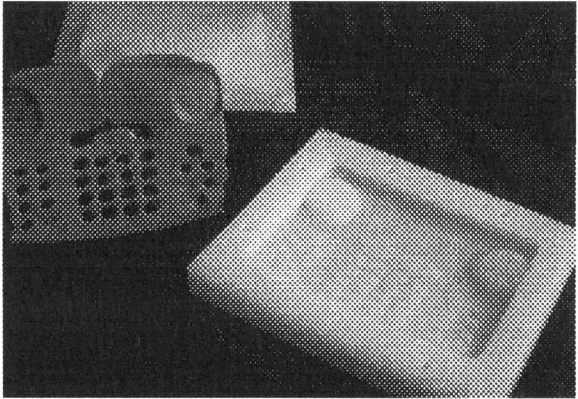

Figure 5.15. The Direct Injection Mould and one of the Moulded Parts.

Conclusions

The results of the tests are shown in the picture in figure .

The part seems too big for this process. To fill the mould completely, a very high pressure is required. Since the mould need to have a relative low surface temperature, the plastic freeze before it fills the cavity. Increased temperature on the injected plastic resulted in very high shrinkage factor.

The test might have suffered from being controlled by an operator trained to tune a steel tool, a plastic insert has to be handled extremely carefully.

5.6 EXAMPLES

5.6.1 Flygt (lost LOM)

ITT Flygt make submergeable pumps. Sub scale tests are done to test different properties of the pumps. The scale models are frequently made using FFF to reduce the manufacturing cost. The scale tests are executed to measure the efficiency of a pump and to measure other data like pressure and flow. ITT Flygt have different analysis programmes for optimization of the pump geometry, but the final verification has to be done with tests. One method is factor tests. With these systematic tests it is possible to find out how different design parameters affect the performance of the pump and how the design parameters affect/interact with each other.

A vortex pump is an open pump design that is often used as a low price pump. To verify the performance of a vortex pump ITT Flygt have chosen to combine FFF, lost wax castings and factor tests.

The following parameters were varied:

- the thickness of the blades
- the number of blades
- the curvature of the blades

Each parameter was varied on two levels, totally eight configurations. There was also one extra pump made with all the variables on an average level. This reference pump was used to verify the linearity of the test.

By making the solid model parametric, all the different configurations could be made in one CAD model. The models were manufactured by a LOM machine. The models were mounted on a wax tree and were used as wax patterns. After the burn out process the pump wheels were cast in stainless steel. Since the lost wax process is capable of holding tight tolerances and a high surface finish, the only machine operation required was centre drilling. Thereafter the pumps were tested and the results evaluated.

5.6 EXAMPLES

Figure 5.16. A LOM Pattern and the Castings.

5.6.2 Rapid Tooling for Wax Moulding

The Solid Ground Curing process from Cubital operated by SINTEF Production Engineering, is very often used for rapid production of moulds for different casting processes. Tooling for sand casting or tooling for making wax pattern for investment casting is most common.

This is an application story showing how Rapid Tooling in combination with investment casting gave birth to an impeller for the Swedish company ITT Flygt.

ITT Flygt is a company represented In more than 100 countries all over the world. They are among the leading producer of submersible pumps. The pumps are known world-wide for their long service life , even in the most adverse operating conditions. ITT Flygt originated the revolutionary, close-couple, submersible, motor driven, waste-water pump. Since 1948 ITT Flygt has been in the forefront in new developments. They have the same need as the rest of the industry to reduce the development time for new pump designs. New products from ITT Flygt is designed by use of 3 D CAD. The main production process for pump components is different casting processes, with sand casting as the major one.

At the end of '94, ITT Flygt was in progress of bringing a new design from it's digital 3 D environment to reality. They had a urgent need for tree samples of an impeller, scaled to 87 % compared to a full size impeller. This impeller was for a waste water pump, capable for handling large solid particles without problems. Such pumps are equipped with a shrouded single-channel impeller running in a volute. The shape and the size of the channel minimise clogging, and therefore make the pump ideal for waste water containing large solid particles.

The designer at ITT Flygt wanted to se if it was possible to make this impeller by investment casting. They turned to Trustor Precision Components, TPC, a Swedish investment casting foundry. Material requirements for the impeller was stainless steel, a standard material for TPC. SINTEF and TPC have been co-operating from time to time in applying time compression techniques for bringing complex cast made by investment casting process as fast as possible to the customer. TPC with their skills on investment casting and SINTEF with their ability to turn a complex design into a mould, and reproduce this mould as a Rapid Tooling part in their SGC process, is a strong team.

Prior to this impeller story, SINTEF had provided TPC with several Layer by Layer produced tooling for casting wax parts. These acrylic tools has proved to function for wax casting with some limitations and restrictions. Compared to normal wax tooling made in aluminium, a layer by layer manufactured tool are made in an acrylic like plastic material. They are easy to identify by having the stair step effect from the layer by layer process. After the Rapid Tool is produced and before the first test cast can be done, a finishing job has to be applied to the surfaces in the cavity, eliminating most of the stair step effect form the process. In the SGC process at SINTEF the normal layer thickness is 0.15 mm. For most practical cases, this is an accepted value. When preparing a wax tool made in a layer by layer process, this after work can take from hour to days. When the job is done, it can be hard to distinct a RP made tool from a conventional made tool by comparing wax part after.

There is another important process parameter who will influence on the cycle time for the wax casting, and that is the heat transfer capacity in the plastic material compared with the much higher heat transfer capacity in a tool made of aluminium. The mould made of plastic has to be closed for a much longer time, to be sure that the wax is solidified before opening the mould a removing the core parts. From what is experienced the holding time can be in the order of 4 to 5 times longer in a mould made of plastic compared to a conventional mould made of aluminium.

When using a Layer by Layer technique for making tooling for wax casting, we are talking about a process for making short runs, depending of part size and complexity. Again the speed of the Rapid Prototyping technique is an interesting and important parameter, and will be the driving force in further developing of this concept.

Turning back to the impeller story and the CAD work. SINTEF was responsible for adapt the 3D CAD geometry from ITT Flygt to the casting process, and for the casting of the wax itself. It was impossible to cast the part as one item, therefore the impeller was divided in three parts, a top part looking like a disc, a centre part consisting of the blade itself, and the bottom part also in shape like a disc. Each part was provided with male / female connection pins for ease of .assembly

5.6 EXAMPLES

5.6.2.1 A big part - almost to big

The impeller was scaled to 87 % compared with full scale. Even when scaled, it was big. The diameter was close to 400 mm and the height was almost 200 mm. Caste weight was almost 50 kg. Totally three moulds was made, one for each of the three wax parts the impeller was devided in. The size of the mould was outside the total working envelope of the Cubital process. A cut and glue together process had to be done on each part. The reason for that is that the maximum working area in the x-y direction in the SGC process is 480x340. With a part size measuring almost 400 mm in diameter, we were outside the limitation in the y direction.

When all the parts assembled and the finishing work done, it was time to pour wax into the cavity. Wax was melted at approx. 73 C, and the casting was done by normal gravity force. A lot of holes was taken in the upper part of each mould to give way for the trapped air to evacuated easily. We experienced a good accuracy on each wax part and it was quite easy to do the assembly. The positioning devices functioned OK and the join between each wax part was good.

One bottleneck to overcome when making wax part at one remote location compared to where the foundry is located, is the transportation and the big risk for damaging the brittle wax details. In this case is was not to risky because the wall thickness in the impeller parts was quite big compared. When the parts arrived at TPC they became a little bit surprised by the size of the impeller. It was by size and weight at the limit for their process equipment.

ITT Flygt got their impellers caste in stainless steel, a little bit later than the original schedule for the delivery, but in time to do the test they needed to perform before going to the next step in their product development activity.

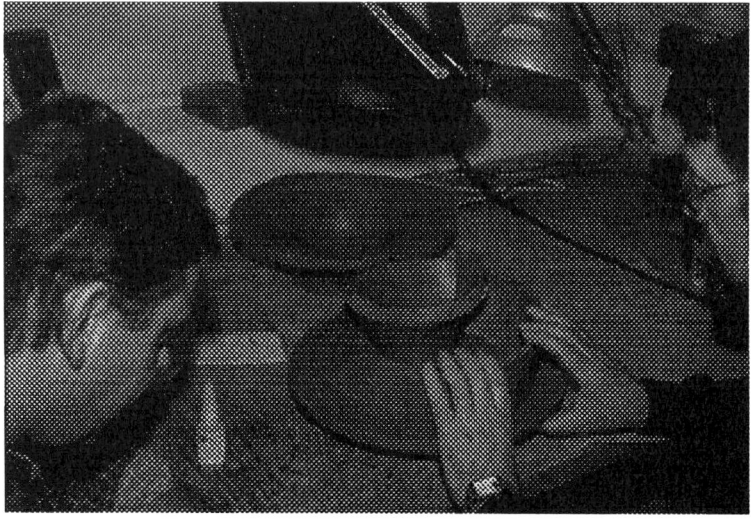

Figure 5.17. Assembling of each Wax Segment to Form a Complete Impeller.

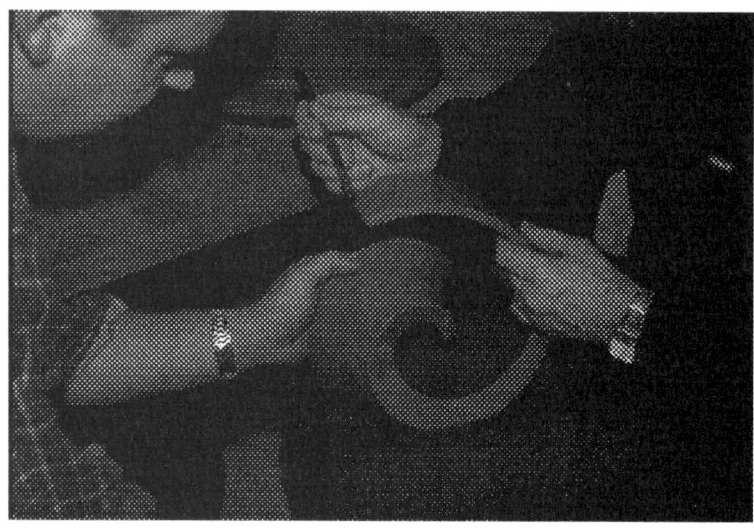

Figure 5.18. The Blade was Twisted More than 360 Degrees.

Figure 5.19. The Complete Wax Impeller after Assembly.

5.6 EXAMPLES

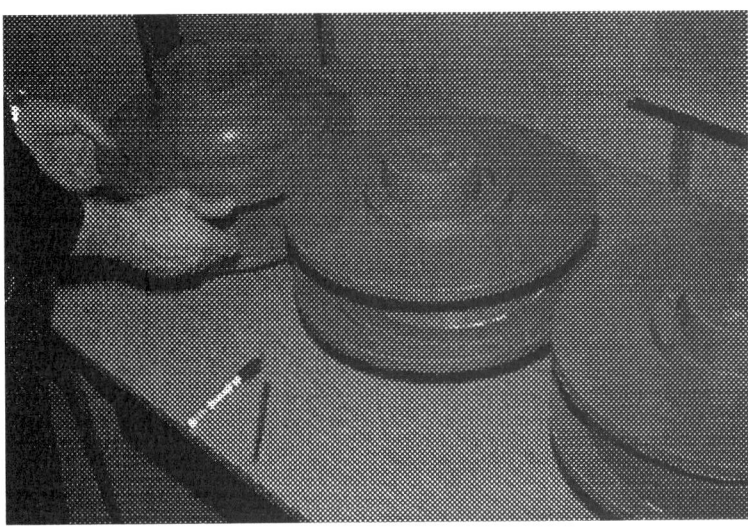

Figure 5.20. Three Impellers Ready for Shipment to the Foundry.

5.6.3 Case Study from IVF Stockholm

Volvo Aero make components for the European space industry. To test the possibility of making cast and then waxed structures an outlet manifold was selected. The patterns were made in the SLS machine of IVF-KTH with 2 and 3 mm wall thickness. The part consisted of an inner and an outer shell. These were joined by a number of guide vans used to direct the airflow out of the turbine. This made the casting sensitive to a uniform cooling and good gating to avoid distortions. The parts were cast by TPC in Hallstahammar in Inconel 638 with good results.

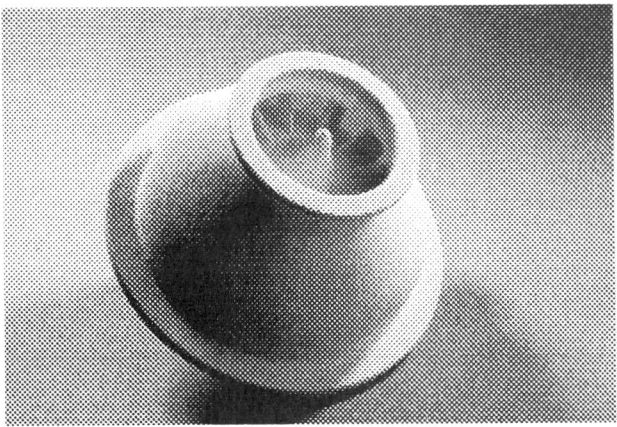

Figure 5.21. The SLS Part.

Figure 5.22. The Casting.

6 DIGITISING AND LMT IN REENGINEERING

6.1 REVERSE ENGINEERING

Reverse engineering is a general description of a process where the aim is the creation of a computer model by measuring an already existing physical model. The computer model will then be used for manufacturing of new physical models, maybe in other materials and maybe after the computer model has been modified. It may also be used for manufacturing a tool for making the physical parts.

The typical situation where this would be desirable is when the actual product was never designed in 3D CAD - either it is an old part, e.g. a spare part is required, or it is a conceptual model that was hand-made by a designer or model maker. Of course it may also be a competitor's product that is being studied. Another reason for reverse engineering is if modifications have been made manually to a physical part and the CAD model subsequently needs to be updated. Especially where the aesthetics and/or the ergonomics of the product are important issues, this may be the most rapid way to reach a good result.

The combination of reverse engineering and RP has promises of offering a fast way of running through several iterations especially in those cases where tests on the physical parts, changes and new tests is the way to develop the product. Design errors could be avoided at an early stage and more optimised solutions could be the result.

However the reverse engineering process is dependent on adequate solutions in two fields: the measuring/digitising and the organisation of the measured data.

6.2 DIGITISING

Several digitising methods have been developed recently and new improvements are often presented. To the traditional co-ordinate measuring machines have been added laser scanners, moiré devices, manual touch-probe devices and others. The output of all these devices is x, y and z co-ordinates for points or rather point clouds.

The traditional co-ordinate measuring machines are being somewhat adapted to better correspond to reverse engineering requirements. Improved control systems facilitate measurement of undefined objects in optional planes. Also new machines exist where the probe has been replaced by a laser device making it a non-contact solution. Still it is a slower process than some other methods.

There are two kinds of laser digitises: point and line range sensors. Both utilise laser light that is emitted and then reflected off the surface of the object to be measured, back to a CCD unit. The point range sensor is more accurate but a lot slower than the line range sensor. The latter is very efficient for surfaces where the aesthetic issue is the most important. In both cases the result is dependant on the surface quality of the object and special treatment may be necessary. A more important restriction is that concavities and hidden areas require particular attention and may be impossible to measure at all by these methods. A human face can be successfully digitised but the ears cause problems.

Moiré devices are highly accurate as well as fast. In fact the high number of points that are very quickly created may be a problem in itself to handle in the subsequent conversion and data processing. Present equipment can only handle small objects, max. 100 mm.

Manual or semi-manual devices exist with different, both mechanical and light-based, types of sensors. Though less expensive, a draw-back is that the result is more dependent on the skill of the operator. They are also slow, on the other hand more suited to an interactive way of digitising where the operator may add topology to the scan data.

X-ray techniques originating from medical applications are now used for digitising of mechanical parts too. An advantage is that interior cavities that can't be reached by most methods are also captured although with limitations - the x-rays don't penetrate very far if it is a metal part.

A very special new type of digitiser could be described as an inverted RP machine. The object is encased in a block of epoxy. Layer by layer the block is milled away and for each layer the exposed surface of the part is scanned using a flat-bed scanner. A big advantage is that all interior cavities otherwise hard to digitise get scanned simultaneous to the contour surface of the part. The draw-back is obviously that the part gets destroyed.

6.3 MODEL CREATION

The efficiency of the scanning systems in producing a huge number of points is already high, but the real challenge is yet to be solved: to automatically organise these data in such a way that a consistent CAD model, which is topological meaningful to its further use, can easily be created.

A CAD system and a digitising system look differently upon the same geometry. In the simple case of a straight edge, the digitising system uses a large number of points to approximate the edge while the CAD system requires only two points to exactly define the same edge. Even more important, the digitising system knows no difference between points belonging to the edge or not, while the CAD system can make use of the fact that it is handling an edge.

Software packages exist which make the transition from point clouds to CAD models easier for the user, e.g. there are algorithms to filter points and smooth curves and surfaces. There are also a number of direct interfaces between digitising systems and CAD systems which facilitate the transfer of point clouds. In general though a lot of effort and time is required from a skilled CAD person in order to make digitising data into a CAD model ready for further use. However, if what is required is mainly a way of quickly producing a new physical model by means of RP, the complete CAD model may not be necessary. A simplified, triangular model could be sufficient.

6.4 CASE

An example of successful combination of reverse engineering and RP is the production of investment cast steel impellers where the origin was not a CAD model but one, hand made, impeller blade and the corresponding body. It was made in the following steps:

- Partly manual manufacture of impeller body with one blade
- Digitising in co-ordinate machine
- CAD modelling from point data and defined boundary curves
- Design of master patterns of impeller body and blade
- RP manufacture (Cubital) of master patterns of impeller body and blade
- Manufacture of epoxy wax mould using master patterns
- Injection moulding of wax patterns
- Assembly of wax patterns - impeller body and 5 blades
- Investment casting of impeller

7 COMMUNICATION

7.1 FAST COMMUNICATIONS - A NECCESSITY IN PRODUCT DEVELOPMENT

Increased application of 3D CAD and LMT technology in industry means increased demands on the ability to transmit this information between the companies and R&D-organizations participating in the different stages of the product development process. In a short term perspective it is particularly important that the companies with 3D CAD-constructions, which do not have LMT-equipment themselves for producing models and prototypes, can use high velocity network for transmission of digital information between companies, LMT-centres and specialists such as foundaries and toolmakers on whom they are dependent.

Efforts were spent in organizing and establishing a functional ISDN-network between the participating Scandinavian LMT-centres at the very start of the project planning. This ISDN-network was planned to ensure a fast and safe transmission of test, sound and images as well as enabling a quick and cost-effective transmission of a large quantity of data between LMT-centres, specialists and companies.

As has been noted earlier, companies should strive for concurrent engineering instead of sequential. Concurrent engineering demands that data and information concerning the development of the product must always be available at the same time for the different parties participating in the product development process. It must also be possible to arrange meetings quickly between the different parties to enable discussion about various alternative shaping, detailed questions etc.

Constructions done in 3D CAD must be able to be quickly transmitted to one of the available LMT-centres or LMT service firms for the developing of prototypes.

When necessary one must also be able to discuss and confirm adjustments needed for the prototype to be used in in the next step, for example for casting or other tool development.

Without effective communication for transmission of blue-prints and construction papers between the various parties - which are often situated at a distance from each other - and good possibilities, despite the distance, to discuss possible alterations then there is a risk that some of the advantages of LMT-technology disappear when information is transmitted between the parties concerned.

The ISDN network must be able to ensure a fast and safe transmission of digital information as well as being able to quickly and effectively spread knowledge and make it possible for the participating companies and LMT-centres to have necessary discussions. If possible this should be done via picture-phones or videos, thus saving time and cutting out misunderstandings and doubts at an early stage of the product development process.

Against this background it was decided at the planning of the project that those participating in the LMT-project should test different ways of hurrying up and simplifying the communication and exchange of information between the various parties. The measures taken and tried have, besides using Internet for transferring files and creating Bulletin Board Systems, BBS, simplified availability and increased service to the LMT-projects members and customers and may be used by ISDN for transmitting files and video conferences.

7.2 ISDN AND VIDEO CONFERENCES SOME FUNDAMENTAL FACTS

A video conference is easiest described as a meeting or conversation, face to face, with help of sound and image communication where the participitants can both see and hear each other. Such video conferences can take place between different parties irrespective of distance, as long as the necessary equipment and network services are available.

For video conferences today the choice depends on the transmission quality desired as well as the price. Network service giving different communication velocity depends on these two factors. All the group systems for video conferences available on the market use a digital network. Since some years back now digital networks, such as ISDN, have been a matter of course when transmitting large amounts of data and for video conferences. The reason for this is that ISDN is a public service which is easily available, with relative low costs for connecting and usage.

There are two different types of video conference systems. One is a desk top system suitable for all types of PCs and UNIX-work stations. The other is a group system which demands a specially equiped room or studio for the video

7.2 ISDN AND VIDEO CONFERENCES

conference. A screen, camera microphone and codek per person or group are necessary to set up a video conference. The codek is the only bit of equipment here which is not a standard product today. It is the actual brain of the image system and is necessary for converting the analogue and digital signals as the network usually uses digital signals. The converting technology is in the actual codek, thus making it the systems most vital part. The codek serves as an interface between image and sound equipment and transmission in the communication network.

The various codek manufacturers use different principles to compress information. The systems using the standard H.320 can almost always communicate with each other without problems irrespective if it's a desk top or group system. The codek can to various degrees comprise machine and programme or sometimes, not so often, only programme. The quality of the image and the synchronization of the sound both depend almost entirely on the capacity of the codek

7.3 COLLABORATIVE COMPUTING

Working in a network -collaborative computing - is becoming more and more important as the need for more people to effectively work integrated with each other becomes more common. Desk top systems make this possible principally in interactive collaboration in actual time between different members of, for example a project team, product development group or other types of work groups.

Desk top systems have other functions than just video conferences for interactive personal communication in acutal time. They make it possible for two or more to work in the the same document at the same time. It is possible here to share blue prints, presentations and estimations with others. This is known as interactive applications. The desk top systems of today are ordinary work stations or PCs which have been supplemented with equipment for video conferences. The systems on the market usually have programmes suitable for interative applications. One problem however is that these systems are specific to the suppliers thus limiting the possibility of collaborting with others who do not have the same desk top system.

7.4 HOW DOES IT WORK?

Our ambitions at the start of the project were high regarding the possibilities for gaining fast and effective transmission of all types of information and above all the possibilities for collaborative computing. Some of the parties taking part in the project had however already obtained ISDN-subscriptions and video equipment for other purposes and partners. The other participants also chose their equipment for the functions they thought important for communication and collaboration between themselves and others outside the project.

The problem we met was that the "state of art" regarding the interactive applications in the desk top systems meant that the different machines were not wholly compatible with each other. This due to the fact that intergated applications needed for collaborative computing are made up of two or more of the following parts:

- file transmission
- still transmission
- image transmission in actual time
- video conferences
- video recording/playbacks
- share-screen
- whiteboard

Various suppliers programmes were not compatible enough to allow the different parties in the project, independent of the equipment suppliers, to make use of all the integrated applications. The possibility for collaborative computing was therefore limited to those parties which had equipment from the same suppliers. Communication and the interactive collaboration have thus become mainly two way, point to point.

File transmission of documents, blue prints and production papers of different types between different types of equipment gave virtually no problem if they were saved in a file form which could be controlled by the equipment belonging to the other partners. This also applied to still transmissions.

Video conferences and simultaneous video recording/playbacks in actual time were also possible, independent of the video equipment used, as long as the same compression technology was used, for example H.320. Meetings between many and various participants were also possible, irrespective of distance. It should however be noted that the quality of both image and sound was much higher if the equipment used came from the same supplier.

Share-screens, that is to say devided screens or devided window applications, would make it possible for two or more PCs to show the same screen image at the

7.4 HOW DOES IT WORK?

same time. This would enable two users to share a screen and work on the same document or estimation at the same time although they are in different places. Alterations made by one of the users would be noted at once. Devided screens can be implemented in two different ways. One is that both persons involved watch each others screen while one makes the alterations. The other is that both persons make the alterations at the same time.

Devided whiteboards would make it possible to mark or draw on a screen with the help of a mouse and this would be seen at the moment of drawing on the other screen. This concept is like the traditional whiteboard where everyone has a different coloured pencil to make their own notes/drawings.

These types of functions are included in almost all the interactive applications in desk top systems. They are, however still supplier-specific, which means that the receiver must have the same equipment to be able to work interactively in a network. Different equipment from various suppliers in the project made it impossible to work interactively with devided screens or whiteboards.

To conclude we must point out that we have had a much greater ambition regarding the possibilities for collaborative computing than "state of art" has allowed. The possibility of being able, with the help of IT, to discuss details in construction at product development and product manufacturing, at a distance and interactively between different parties, has been dependent on how the suppliers equipment and products have been compatible with others.

If we finally, however, see to the endeavours the international collaboration organizations and standarizing organisations have made in this region then we can say that in the not too distant future everyone - theoretically - will be able to contact and collaborate with each other through collaborative computing.

8. INDUSTRIAL CASE STUDIES

8.1 NEW TECHNOLOGY AND FLOW OF INFORMATION A CONDITION FOR DEVELOPMENT OF DEMANDING PRODUCTS

The company Industrial Produktservice AS (IPS) was established in Levanger, Norway, in 1979 specialising in mechatronics. We offer design and construction of mechanics in electronic products, prototypes, small series and products well prepared for industrial production. Our employees possess substantial knowledge within product development for the electronics industry and other industry requiring the same kind of expertise.

For IPS the product development from drawing-board to CAD started as early as 1985, and since 1993 3D CAD has been used for visualisation, design, rapid prototyping, documentation and tooling. Our constructors are highly experienced in 3D modelling and more than 5500 work hours have been carried out using these tools (Nov. 1995). This experience enables us to exploit the equipment very efficiently.

Product development is a strategic activity. The products' functionality, design and production cost are of decisive importance for the company's competitiveness in the market. With short and intensive economic fluctuations the requirements for quality, flexibility and productivity are stricter. A condition for survival with global competitiveness is short through-put times for all activities and processes. A steady process flow is required during the development time as well as for production of new products.

The technical development with regard to information has enabled a reduced through-put time. In addition to keeping the company's most important resource, the employees, updated, we must also be up to date with regard to the necessary computer tools. The objective of IPS is also to be the leading company with regard to the implementation of new technology and processes.

8.1.1 Design and product development

Good communications is a precondition for succeeding with the product development. Here we do not only think of the written or spoken word, but of a communication model which can serve as a means or tool to provide all interested parties with sufficient information so that the decision makers have enough information to make the right decisions. Being able to provide a 3D conceptual design early in the process can be of vital importance to the project's decision makers.

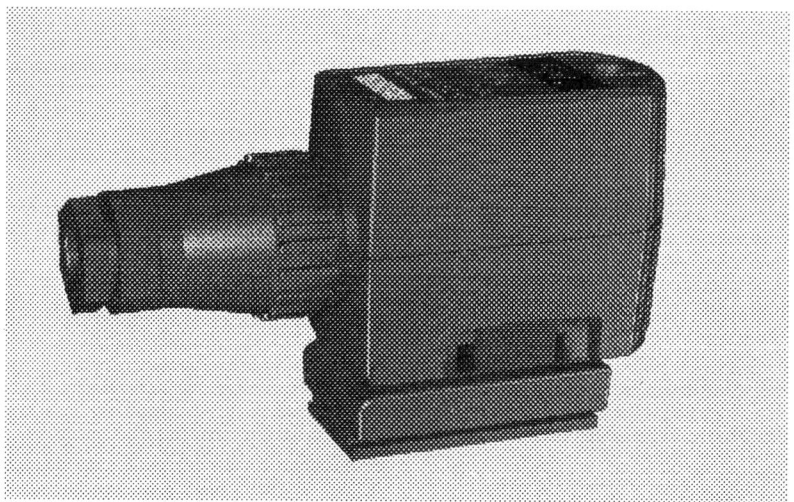

Figure 8.1. Example of a 3D Design of «Coupler» for the Company Fieldbus International (FINT).

The form and function of the products are an expression of the company's strategy. The contents of this strategy is therefore an important condition for profit and success.

It is in this technical and commercial context that the design of the product becomes important, by meeting the customer's requirements with regard to simplicity, safety and time saving.

A good design stimulates the user's immediate conception of the product's distinctive character and usefulness. Product development is frequently dependent on a number of multidiciplinary factors which often lies outside the designer's field of work. To be able to master the technological aspect it is necessary to know the connection between materials, production processes and the shaping potential the material holds.

By exploiting these possibilities ethically the creation process will be directed towards an integration in the product. This integration is the key to a rational design of the product, with exploitation of the technical possibilities which can be found in high technology production and materials.

8.1 NEW TECHNOLOGY AND FLOW OF INFORMATION

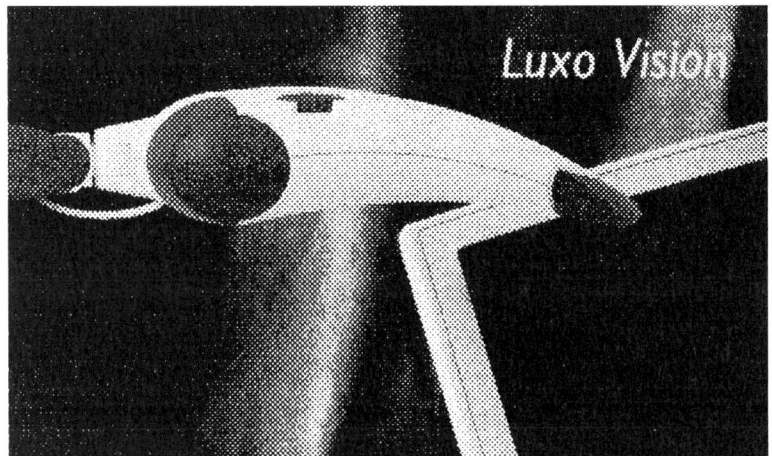

Figure 8.2. Desk Lamp "Luxo Vision" fra Jac Jacobsen.

IPS has experience from a number of projects where the requirement for industrial design has been very challenging and the company collaborates with several qualified industrial designers.

A lot of projects presuppose the use of 3D tools to be able to meet the designer's wish for «complete freedom» with regard to form. 3D curved surfaces which previously could not be defined are now widely used in more and more projects. An example of such a demanding design is Jac Jacobsen's desk lamp «Luxo Vision».

Product designers are only limited by their own creativity. Creativity can be viewed both as a tool and as a state of mind.

To IPS this is a trump card and very important to its developmental work, a thorough design enables a very short way to the finished product.

IPS does not have its own products or production equipment and is therefore totally free in its choice of solutions and processes.

Integrated functions and new production technology make processing, joining and assembly much simpler and provide a unique chance to save time and money.

In recent years IPS has developed a number of various products for Norwegian industrial enterprises. We can provide conceptual solutions for the entire product, design, drafting and documentation.

Calculation of materials and stress factors, air flow and cooling, shock and vibration dimensioning and quite frequently screening, are among other things included in the design work. We verify calculations with regard to measurements and clarify all basic conditions in the design at an early stage during the design work. Our designs shall be prepared and tailored for the final production process.

For instance, for precast parts (light metal or plastic) the following points shall be well prepared: choice of material, surface, gating and feeding, shrink and sink, draft angle, parting plane, pull direction for jaws in tooling for injection moulding.

For sheet steel solutions advantages and disadvantages with regard to choice of material shall be defined, possibilities and limitations in the chosen production processes like punching, laser cutting etc. Application of well established routines for design control is an important part of the work and constitute the basis for the right quality in agreement with specifications.

With a 3D based project implementation we have obtained a very powerful tool for construction of mechanics and we are very pleased with the results we have achieved; a significant saving of time and elimination of error sources.

8.1.2 Prototypes

Surveys show that 80% of a product's quality and 70% of the costs in product development arise in the developmental stages. Surveys also show that a 6-month delay in the marketing of a product may result in a 30% loss of earnings during the products life time.

An efficient project management, the right techniques and 3D computer technology during the development phase can be decisive to ensure the quality and reduce the time and costs.

Rapid prototyping is a new technology which IPS has applied in many projects. This is prototype production directly from a 3D solid model and this technology has revolutionised the manufacture of prototypes.

The IPS involvement in the NOR-LMT project, with four departments/colleges and 40 companies, has contributed to the fact that IPS at any time is up dated on everything that happens within rapid prototyping.

IPS is co-operating with a number of prototype suppliers and in a later stage potential manufacturers of the product, which make the prototype close to the industrialised solution. In this way the prototype contributes to a valuable design verification and functional testing.

8.1.3 Industrialisation

Industrialisation is the area in the product development process in which the tendency to be less thorough is greatest. The prototype seems to be all right and the company is tempted to start serial production without sufficient tools and documentation.

8.1 NEW TECHNOLOGY AND FLOW OF INFORMATION

Figure 8.3. Cubital Model of «Coupler» was Produced at SINTEF Production Engineering while Vacuum Casted Parts were Produced at Elektrolux Rapid Development.

Figure 8.4. Mount, Connector Unit for «Coupler» was Produced as an RP Model at the Danish Technological Institute.

Without a thoroughly considered industrialisation of the product the company will make prototypes with high service costs and with complaints and a dubious reputation in the market as a result.

IPS works out a complete documentation for serial production which among other things includes drawings of all details, joining and assembly, labels, technical documentation, parts lists, packaging etc. Machining data for production tools for plastic and metals etc. can be extracted from 3D and 2D geometry. This information can be provided to the suppliers in the market.

In most projects IPS is also responsible for the follow-up of the various sub-suppliers involved in the project.

IPS carries out control and identifies possible errors and provides corrective measures to all pre series production. This in turn will lead to a correction of the tooling itself at an early stage. When the production has started a progress control is carried out to check that all defined processes are effected.

> Tore Sæther
> IPS AS (Industrial Produktservice AS)
> Helga den Fagresgt. 8 B
> N-7600 Levanger
> Telephone: +47 74 08 94 00
> Telefax: +47 74 08 08 27

8.2 STEP OVERVIEW AND CURRENT STATUS. AN ASSISTANCE IN EVALUATING STEP

8.2.1 Summary

This brief introduction to STEP is written for STEP novices. In providing an overview of this standardisation activity it may be a basis for the evaluation of STEP as a method for the digital representation and exchange of product data in a computer integrated manufacturing and engineering (CIME) environment. Typical CIME-scenarios for the use of STEP-like technologies are, therefore, presented. The benefits of applying standards instead of proprietary solutions are briefly described. The basic idea behind STEP, the product model concept, is discussed before the final walk through of the standard itself.

8.2.2 Definitions

STEP, the Standard for the Exchange of Product Model Data, is as its name suggests, an international standard since 1994, for the digital representation and the digital exchange of product model information. A product model is ideally a complete description of a product. A product may be a tangible object such as a car, or it may be, e.g., a software product. Complete description means that all views of both the different contributors to the product and the users of the product are represented.

8.2.3 Scenarios for the Application of STEP

What may such a complete digital representation be good for? One may consider at least three beneficial uses within CIME:

8.2 STEP OVERVIEW

- systems integration;
- inter-company communication;
- product life-cycle support.

All three uses cover requirements that arise from increasing pressure for short lead times in product development and production and for improved product quality.

The characteristics of systems integration are the reuse of data. A model created in a CAD-system is partly needed in the finite element analysis of the model. The creation of the CAD-model and its analysis are often done by two distinct systems. The geometry that is needed for the analysis is due to the lack of other sharing mechanisms manually regenerated. The direct and automatic reuse of the CAD-model would avoid redundant model creation which is not only little cost-effective, but also error-prone.

The needs in inter-company collaboration are quite similar to the ones just described. The main difference is that the individual companies do not have control over the systems that they shall communicate with. Whereas it is possible within a company to select systems that fit to each other, inter-company collaboration depends on a common exchange format and on the quality of the systems interfaces. This is maybe the most significant application area for a standard for data exchange like STEP.

Finally there is the company specific requirement of product management. Documenting the complete life-cycle of a product is not only advantageous for the development of new related products. Complete documentation is also increasingly required by the authorities. For this, product related data needs to be integrated into one product model. This may be achieved using a single consistent data model such as the one in STEP.

8.2.4 Motivation for a Standard

The motivation for using a digital product representation should be distinguished from the motivation for using an international standard for this purpose. The three scenarios described above could be implemented by different concepts and within each concept by either proprietary or standards solutions. Among the motivations for STEP is the outstanding value of product data a manufacturing company. All its knowledge and experience are represented by the product and - as nowadays electronic data processing is common: by its digital representation. However, the tools for processing data are often by far as long lasting as products and data themselves. It could happen that your product was to be maintained for 40 years whereas the software to maintain it with, will loose support after 20 years. In offshore industries data need to be available for up to 70 years.

Provided a comprehensive international standard that is acknowledged by the system vendors, data could be exploited as long as there are interfaces to the international format. STEP will hopefully reach this stage of a long lasting standard. It would then typically be included as a technical annex into development contracts.

8.2.5 The Product Model Concept

The product model is the kernel of an integration concept that focuses upon product data, opposed to other approaches that focus upon integration by user interface or by control and communication. The data approach relies on the input from the user, i.e., from manufacturing companies, only to a minor degree from system vendors (except when the software itself is dealt with as a product).

STEP favours data integration. The standard provides a generic product model. The kernel of this model contains objects such as product, product version, product category, product definition, and product context. A product may have a geometric description or even several ones, such as a surface description and a solid description. Also other characteristics of the product or its development may be assigned to the kernel of the product model. Examples of such characteristics are material information, finite element input data and result data, tolerances, and visual presentation attributes. New characteristics may be added to the existing STEP model as requirements arise.

8.2.6 The STEP Structure

STEP is the unofficial name for some of the work of sub-committee 4 in the technical committee 184 of ISO (International Organisation of Standardisation). The result of STEP is a series of documents that all together establish the standard ISO 10303. Each document represents one Part of the standard and is identified by a Part number. The complete name of a Part is: ISO 10303-<Part number>.

The STEP approach does not only describe the product model itself. The different Parts are grouped to cover the following topics:

> Part 1:   - Overview and fundamental principles;
> Parts 11 to 19 :   - Description methods;
> Parts 21 to 29 :   - Implementation methods;
> Parts 31 to 39 :   - Conformance testing methodology and framework;
> Parts 41 to 99 :   - Integrated resources: Generic resources;
> Parts 101 to 199: - Integrated resources: Application resources;

8.2 STEP OVERVIEW

>Parts 201 to 299:   - Application protocols;
>Parts 301 to 399:   - Abstract test suites.
>Parts 501 and up : - Application Interpreted Constructs.

The different groups are defined in more detail in the following chapters.

8.2.7 Overview and Fundamental Principles

The overview document (Part 1) provides an introduction into the methods that are applied for the development of the standard. The document structure is introduced, STEP specific terms are defined.

8.2.8 Description Methods

The Parts belonging to the description methods shall specify tools for the development of the standard itself. The only tool available now is the information modelling language EXPRESS (Part 11). A variant of EXPRESS for modelling of instances, EXPRESS-I, has been initiated. The fact that EXPRESS came into being in spite of all the existing modelling languages is a result of the user dependency of STEP. Product modelling depends on the close collaboration of users, i.e., domain experts, and modelling experts. Their communication medium is the information modelling language. Existing languages were considered insufficient with respect to either human readability or modelling capabilities. Another major plus for EXPRESS is that it is computer interpretable. The potential for misinterpreting specifications written in EXPRESS is relatively small compared to specifications written in plain English.

All of the STEP product model Parts are written in EXPRESS.

8.2.9 Implementation Methods

In the context of product data technology it is not only important to specify what to exchange, but also how to do it. STEP currently intends to support data exchange using files and data sharing in databases.

Part 21, Clear text encoding of the exchange structure, controls the format of a STEP-file by providing a mapping from general EXPRESS-constructs to an ASCII-syntax. CAx-system vendors will typically provide processors for the import and export of such files to interface their systems to STEP. Part 21 has reached the status of an international standard.

Part 22, Standard data access interface (SDAI), provides a generic application programming interface to an EXPRESS compliant data repository. The interface itself is specified in EXPRESS. It may be implemented using different programming languages such as FORTRAN, C, and C++. Two kinds of data access are distinguished and are options for implementations:

- entity type specific access (e.g., put/get point);
- entity type independent access (e.g., put/get entity, put/get attribute).

SDAI de-couples applications from EXPRESS repositories. Applications that use SDAI-calls for their data access may work on any database management system as long as SDAI is supported. SDAI can be considered an alternative to embedded SQL.

8.2.10 Conformance Testing Methodology and Framework

A major drawback with existing standards in the domain, such as IGES, has been the lack of certification procedures. The scope of an IGES-processor is not defined. This renders a successful data exchange difficult. An accompanying measure to the product model development in STEP has, therefore, been the specification of a conformance testing methodology and framework. Part 31 describes General Concepts and is approved as an international standard. The following Parts are in work:

> Part 32- Requirements on testing laboratories and clients;
> Part 33- Structure and use of abstract test suites;
> Part 34- Abstract test methods for Part 21 implementations;
> Part 35- Abstract test methods for Part 22 implementations.

8.2.11 Generic Resources

This is the core model of STEP. The different Parts in this series specify how to represent the different characteristics of a generic product. As the title says, these are resources. They are not designed for implementation. The 40-series is the pool from which the models of real life products are deduced. This is done by applying object oriented methods such as object specialisation. The real life models are called Application protocols and are documented in the 200-series.

8.2.12 Application Resources

Not all product characteristics are generic in nature. However, they may nevertheless be of interest to a wider group of products. Electrical connectivity may be an example for this. Such product characteristics are specified and

8.2 STEP OVERVIEW

documented in the 100-series. Also these Parts of the standard shall not be implemented as such, but shall be specialised into application protocols.

The draughting model (Part 101) is for the representation of drawings with dimensions and other annotation and has reached the status of an international standard. The other Parts are (Part 102 has been deleted):

Part 103	- Electrical/electronics connectivity;
Part 104	- Finite element analysis;
Part 105	- Kinematics;
Part 106	- Building Construction Core Model.

8.2.13 Application Protocols

As mentioned above application protocols are the only specifications within ISO 10303 that may be used for STEP conferment implementations. Application protocols (AP) are initiated by domain experts, i.e., by members of the industrial community. APs are developed in collaboration with STEP experts who assist in mapping the industrial requirements to the modelling resources of the 40- and 100-series in order to establish an implementable data model that serves the industrial needs and that is consistent with the whole of STEP. Two application protocols have reached (or are very close to reaching) the status of an international standard:

Part 201	- Explicit draughting;
Part 203	- Configuration controlled design.

Other application protocols that are at different stages of completion are:

Part 202	- Associative draughting;
Part 204	- Mechanical design using boundary representation;
Part 205	- Mechanical design using surface representation;
Part 206	- Mechanical design using wireframe representation;
Part 207	- Sheet metal die planning and design;
Part 208	- Life cycle product change process;
Part 209	- Design through analysis of composite and metallic structures;
Part 210	- Electronic printed circuit assembly, design and manufacture;
Part 211	- Electronics test diagnostics and re manufacture;
Part 212	- Electromechanical plants;
Part 213	- Numerical control process plans for machined parts;
Part 214	- Core data for automotive mechanical design processes;
Part 215	- Ship arrangement;

Part 216 — Ship moulded forms;
Part 217 — Ship piping;
Part 218 — Ship structures;
Part 219 — Dimensional inspection process planning for co-ordinate measuring machines;
Part 220 — Printed circuit assembly manufacturing planning;
Part 221 — Functional data and schematic representation for process plans;
Part 222 — Exchange of design engineering to manufacturing for composite structures;
Part 223 — Exchange of design and manufacturing product information for cast parts;
Part 224 — Mechanical products definition for process planning using form features;
Part 225 — Structural building elements using explicit shape representation;
Part 226 — Ship mechanical systems;
Part 227 — Plant spatial configuration;
Part 228 — Building services;
Part 229 — Forged Parts;
Part 230 — Building services: Heating, ventilation and air conditioning

8.2.14 Abstract Test Suites

A series of its own has been established to define the test conditions for application protocols. There is one abstract test suite per application protocol. An abstract test suite specifies which tests need to be successfully executed by a candidate STEP implementation to qualify for conformance to the application protocol. In general application protocols define several conformance classes, each of which may be the origin of a conformance certificate.

8.2.15 Conclusion

STEP has reached maturity in the areas of shape, configuration control, visual presentation, and draughting. File exchange is the one stable implementation method. STEP has gained considerable support in both Japan, USA, and Europe. Mechanical industry with especially automotive and aircraft is leading the exploitation of the standard. They are followed by electric/electronic, process plant, shipping and building industries. The large user community has caused an increased participation of vendors, not only in specification, but also in implementation activities. Projects from both PDES Inc. (USA), CADDETC (UK),

8.2 STEP OVERVIEW

ProSTEP (Germany), and those funded by the European Commission, such as PRODEX, InterRob, Maritime, Atlas, PISA, ProcessBase etc. are good examples.

STEP is not in industrial use, yet, but it is on its way. It is advantageous for the standard that there is no alternative specification or activity. More and more of those who want to solve problems like systems integration, inter-company collaboration, and product life-cycle support join the STEP community to apply and improve the standard.

8.3 LAERDAL AND THE NOR/LMT PROJECT

Laerdal is concerned with product development, marketing and sale of paramedic products meant for prehospital use. This includes equipment intended for treatment as well as for training. Today the company is leading within this field. Many of the products have proven to be valuable for use in hospitals and for treating of patients in their homes.

Laerdal mostly base their production on exploitation of resources existing within the company. The company applies most techniques for plastic moulding and has its own tooling design section and design workshop. In addition the development department has a well equipped prototype workshop. The electronic production section has employed advanced state-of-the-art assembly techniques. The assembly departments for mechanical assembly utilises robots and automated production lines for mass production. All production of finished goods including packaging is carried out internally in the company. Laerdal also has an in-house printing office for brochures, user manuals and other printed material.

At a very early stage Laerdal saw the potential in using 3D CAD in its development work and due to this decision the development time for several types of products has been significantly reduced. There is a great need for function models and prototypes in the development department. Traditionally these have been machined and/or modelled by a modeller. After introducing 3D CAD we have made use of the Rapid Prototyping processes for many years (Stereolitography, Cubital).

In recent years there has been an increasing need for a simple way to reproduce several prototypes. Normally it takes a lot of time and recourses to produce from 2 - 20 prototypes. Initially in the NOR/LMT project it was decided that Laerdal should establish their own competence within the area of vacuum casting because they realised the potential for reduced time and cost in applying silicon mould and polyurethal casting. This is a method for reproducing accurate details in small runs in a material suitable for function testing. This process is well suited for complex parts even with undercuts.

Traditional tooling for injection moulding is not very cost-effective when producing small series, then you have relatively few products to distribute the costs. This is a problem experienced by many Norwegian companies. During the project period Laerdal has learned a lot about alternative methods for thermoplast tooling for small series production. At the same time a wide network of contacts within Rapid Prototyping and Rapid Tooling has been established.

During the last year Laerdal has invested in HEK Vacuum chambers for casting of polyurethane (PUR) details in silicon moulds as well as HEK metal injection equipment for rapid production of simple and cheap preproduction moulds. Both models presupposes a master model in order to be able to make a mould.

PUR details are used for prototypes for a maximum number of 30 casts per silicon mould. Preproduction moulds are used for trial series. The preproduction moulds provide shape and material flow which is very close to what can be achieved in a steel production tool. Depending on complexity and material these preproduction moulds can at best produce 2000 - 3000 casts.

Figure 8.5. Heart Start 911 Defibrillator Unit as Prototype and Product.

Over the years we have become experienced in using these processes and have achieved very good results. The internal need for rapid tooling is increasing and applying new solutions will be a priority area for Laerdal in the future.

Conclusion: Laerdal has benefited from the NOR/LMT project and is also interested in participating in a similar project relevant to the company.

Ivan Rafoss/Laerdal
Phone: +47 51511794
Fax: +47 51523557

8.4 CERAMIC CORES CAST IN A CORE BOX DIRECTLY GENERATED FROM A DATA MODEL - DOES IT WORK?

8.4.1 Background

Kværner Eureka was one of the Norwegian participants in the NOR-LMT project and in connection with this we were looking for applications suitable for testing the Rapid Prototyping technique in our pump production plant. A water injection pump was found suitable for this experiment. This pump was developed for the *NJORD project*, a part of an offshore oil installation in the North Sea.

We chose this Rapid Prototyping technique to make the core box for casting of the ceramic cores of the runners. The water way in the runner requires great accuracy and cannot be machined. Normally, the core box is manually made by a pattern maker. In this venture we hoped to profit both with regard to time and accuracy at the same time as we gained experience with this new technology.

The runners were to be cast in a separate foundry. Kværner Eureka casts runners with ceramic cores, something which is not customary but gives a smooth and accurate surface. During casting the ceramic core is placed in a sand mould. The sand mould creates the outer surfaces which later are to be machined, while the core creates the water way including the blades.

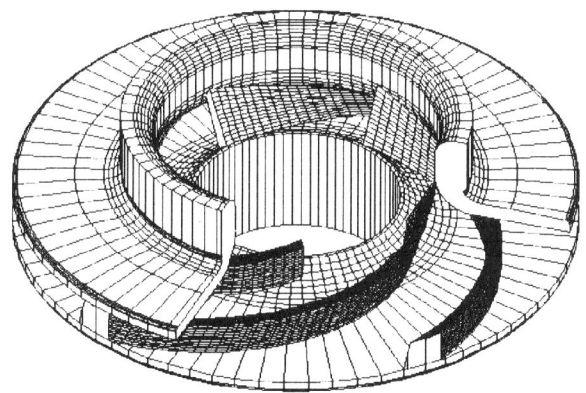

Figure 8.6. Wire Frame of the Finished Runner.

8.4.2 Implementation

The basis for the design of the runners was hand-made drawings made by the American company UCP with which we have a licence. The drawings being hand-made gave room for inaccuracies. The outer shape of the runner is symmetrical and thus easy to make by rotating a simple 2D curve in space. The blades are determined by use of special projecting techniques. The projections are partly used for calculation during the design phase and partly by the pattern maker for design of the physical shape.

First we had to copy the necessary projections to 2D-CAD. Some modifications were made to adjust the runners to fit our pump.

The 2D drawing was further used as basis for the 3D modelling of the blades. Such a 3D model made of 2D projections often reveal less suitable shapes invisible in 2D (too sharp changes of direction etc). Thus the blades were further adjusted before we reached an acceptable form. Figure 1 shows a wire frame of the finished runner.

The core box consists of a fundament which constitutes the inner wall of the water way, blades and a lid which constitutes the outer wall. These three models were sent to SINTEF. SINTEF Production Engineering added a mounting device to each blade, on the 3D CAD model. This mounting device was provided with draft angle. The mounting device was subtracted from the fundament by Boolean operation. This enabled exact positioning of each blade in the mould. The fundament for the blade including the mounting device can, after casting of the core, be removed so that each blade can be pulled out of the ceramics. See Figure 9.6.

SINTEF made plastic models based on these data models and the accuracy was satisfactory. The surface was improved by painting the models. The foundation was somewhat twisted and this was corrected by mounting the fundament to a flat, stiff wooden board.

There was some uncertainty to whether this plastic material was suited for use as mould material. We decided to use the plastic material directly and instead use the master to make castings in a more suited material if the experiment failed. However, the experiment was a success and we were able to proceed without carrying out further casting processes.

The ceramic cores are cast by pouring liquid ceramics into the core box while it rotates. This is to provide a good filling and to avoid air bubbles. The moulds open and the blades are taken out before the ceramics has hardened, then the cores are burnt. In this case the cores turned out fine and there was no problem to use make direct use of the plastic models.

8.4.3 Conclusion

The core box made directly from data models functioned well. Measurements showed that the model was accurate and the plastic models were suitable as moulds for casting of ceramics.

The improved accuracy of the model was most important. Previously the blades have been made by a pattern maker on the basis of 2D projections. Inaccuracies in this 2 dimensional presentation have usually been corrected according to

8.4 CERAMIC CORES CAST IN A CORE BOX

experience and knowledge of the product. Now it was possible to correct such inaccuracies during the 3D CAD modelling. As this model could be generated with such high degree of accuracy we were able to control the end result. Small deviations can influence the result greatly and especially when we are dealing with such high water speeds as in this pump.

High accuracy of the physical model compared to the calculated shape makes it possible to scale pumps with a larger degree of accuracy. When making new pumps we know that the runner which is tested fits well with the calculated 2D projections, and thus these can be scaled with greater accuracy.

Even though the runner is still designed in 2D according to established criteria we experienced that 3D modelling of the blades according to the 2D projections revealed inaccuracies and undesired local deviations. By correcting the 3D model and then again correcting the 2D projections accordingly more accurate design rules for calculation of the water way can be obtained. This opens up for carrying out flow analysis by use of FEM tools.

With regard to the time aspect it was little to be gained by this project; making plastic models directly from data models compared to a pattern maker working according to 2D drawings. But if 3D models are to be made anyway, with the benefits this includes, this direct rapid tooling process will be worth while. By establishing methods for automatic 3D modelling of 2D projections it will be possible to carry out the 3D modelling faster.

The present costs for this technique are higher than for manual model making. We must also take into consideration the fact that there are fewer and fewer pattern makers who are able to do this kind of work. In the future we will do most of our design in 3D CAD systems with the possibility to make direct tooling with short lead times. This project has been of valuable experience to us.

Rune Pettersen/ Kvaerner Eureka AS
Phone: +47 32859289
Fax: +47 32850560

8.5 NEW DIGITISING DEVICE AT HUT

Helsinki University of Technology Lahti Centre has installed a new digitising device (FARO-arm) which can be used in a quality control and measuring of products and in revenge engineering -digitising surfaces and geometry's of work pieces.

The device (Figure 9.7) is a "robot arm" with six joints. Each joint has an optical angle sensor for measuring and calculation of the position of touch probe. The workspace is a ball with diameter 2.4 m but also bigger parts can be measured by moving the device to an other location and using shared reference points. The accuracy is about 0.1 mm in all positions of the arm. Because of the great number of the degree of freedom is it possible to digitise surfaces which are difficult to reach for example with a co-ordinate measuring machine or a laser digitise.

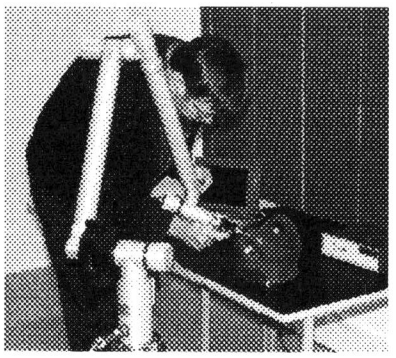

Figure 8.7. FARO Digitising Device.

Figure 8.8. 3D-model (half) of joint.

The device can digitise single points or basic features like lines, circles, spheres etc. The software of the device compensates automatically the radius of the ball probe.

Complex surfaces can be scanned with a free hand or locked planes method. Points or curves which describe the surfaces can be directed into a CAD-program. These points and curves are then used for surface modelling and further for solid modelling. When using a ball probe is it necessary to use an offset function of a CAD program to compensate the ball radius.

The movements of the probe can be monitored on a computer screen during digitising process. The modelling and the digitising processes can be done by turns.

The device is also easy to move and the set-up time is short.

8.5 NEW DIGITISING DEVICE AT HUT

8.5.1 Application Example

One of the case projects at HUT/LC was a joint (Figure 9.8) from the company Sisu Axles. The purpose of this project was to do a 3D-CAD model of the joint. The model was used in casting, FEM analysing and documentation.

The free surfaces of the joint were scanned with the locked planes method and 3D surfaces were modelled based on digitised curves. We went trough the surfaces to a closed surface model which was further turned to a solid model. Machined surfaces were measured and modelled as parametric features. As a result we got a solid model of the joint with parametric features.

All surfaces also inside geometry was be digitised by one fastening. The modelling was done with Pro/Engineer 3D-CAD software and it's Scan tool module.

3D-model was sent as an IGES file to Sisu Axles which is using CATIA-system. The foundry participating in this project is using Pro/Engineer CAD-system. The foundry got the original Pro/E-file.

HUT/Lahti Centre
Jukka Tuomi
Juhani Seppänen

8.6 MATERIAL AND FUNCTION TESTING OF A NEW FOOT CONTROLLER

The purpose of this project was to test the functionality and the material of a new foot controller construction of a Compact unit. Because of the very rapid time schedule of this project it was decided to use RP-technology to make prototypes for these tests.

Planmeca Group is one of the world's leading manufacturers of dental equipment with over 700 employees (-95) and turnover about 750 million FIM (-95). Planmeca Oy manufactures and markets wide range dental products (Figure 9.9) for example digitized and film based imaging systems, intra-oral x-rays, dental units, patient chairs etc.. It exports 95% of its productions to more than 70 countries in Europe, North America and the Far East. Planmeca Oy developes all it s products in 3D-CAD-system and uses regulary RP-technology in its product and production development. They have a good experience almost from all RP-methods and they send a new offer request to RP-offices about once a month.

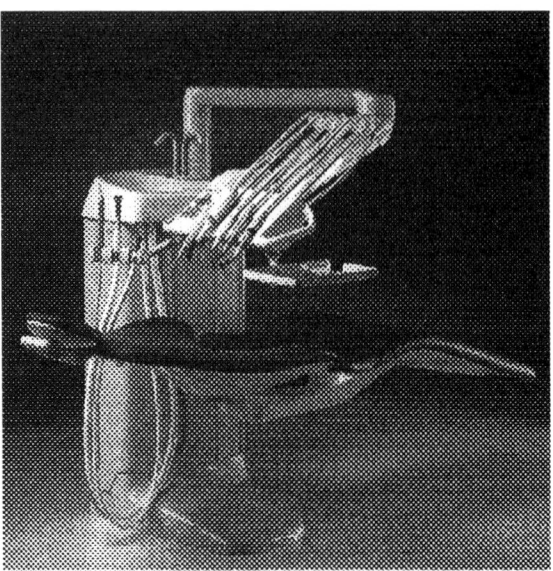

Figure 8.9 The Protsyle Patient Support System.

The Compact unit is a dental equipment, which includes among other things the foot controller. A dentist can use this controller by his foot to control for example the positions of a chair and instrument functions.

Today the coupling arm of this controller is manufactured by cutting from steel and machining. The arm is one kind of lever and its length is about 20 cm (Figure 9.10). In an assembly phase a silicon rubber knob will be mounted on the other end of this arm. The assembly of the foot controller unit includes in addition to mechanical parts also electonic, among other things a circuit board with its sensors. A steel plate mounted on the arm together with the circuit board forms a capasitive sensor, which examins the different positions of the coupling arm.

Injection moulded plastic could be a better material for the arm instead of steel. It could have many advantages for example the number of assembly parts would decrease, many work phases would be left away, the quality would be more constant and also the assembly costs would be lower.

Before starting the manufacturing of the injection mould, it was neccessary to examine part's properties for injection moulding, goodness of the construction, material choice and function of the idea. After 3D-design of the parts and STL-translation offer requests of the coupling arm (two different parts) were sent to RP-offices. The offers were requested from two FDM-operators, one SLS-operator and from the operator which makes prototype molds using direct metal laser sintering process. The parts were made with the SLS-method (IVF-Stockholm) because the new material (50% nylon, 50% fiberglass) which has good

8.6 MATERIAL AND FUNCTION TESTING

strength properties. Also the direct metal laser sintering process was very interesting alternative, where the manufactured RP-model would have been an injection mould instead of a RP-part. The frame of the mould would have been made from aluminium. The delivery would have been consisted only of the injection moulded parts to Planmeca Oy. The seller estimated that with the sintered mould it is possible to manufacture 200 - 300 parts. The seller couldn't however guarantee the life time of this mold even for 50 pieces because of new technology.

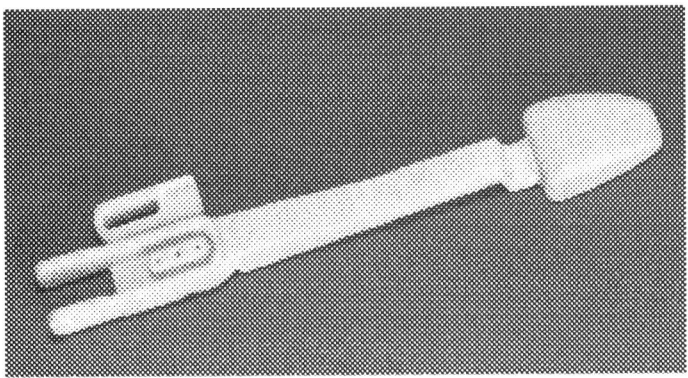

Figure 8.10. The RP-Model of the Coupling Arm.

RP-parts came to Planmeca Oy about in one week after sending the STL-files. The parts were assembled together for the tests on a test bench. The assembly of two RP-parts succeeded with a slight extra work. The tests showed that this new construction of the foot controller made of plastic was not strong enough because the bending was too high. It showed also that there is need to improve the basic idea of the construction.

In this project the use of RP-technology instead direct injection mould manufacturing saved much time and money. The further development will continue on the basis of this experience.

Veli-Pekka Vesanen/Planmeca Oy
Juhani Seppänen/HUT,Lahti Centre

8.7 WATER JET IMPELLER

The purpose of this project was to develop the manufacturing process of a water jet impellers so that they could be casted in one piece using rapid prototyping and investment casting methods. This project was done in co-operation with Helsinki University of Technology/Lahti Centre and the companies FFJet Ltd and Sacotec Precision Castings. It's phases were tooling of a prototype impeller, digitising, 3D modelling, rapid prototyping, soft tooling and investment casting.

FFJet Ltd is located in Kokkola, Finland and belongs to KaMeVa group. It is specialised in the production of water-jet propulsion and design and manufacture of demanding propulsion modules. The patch size is typically 10 - 20 impellers. The customers are mostly maritime authorities, coast guards and defence forces in various countries. Sacotec Precision Castings is an investment casting foundry in Riihimäki, Finland which produces metallic casted parts to Finnish and foreign customers.

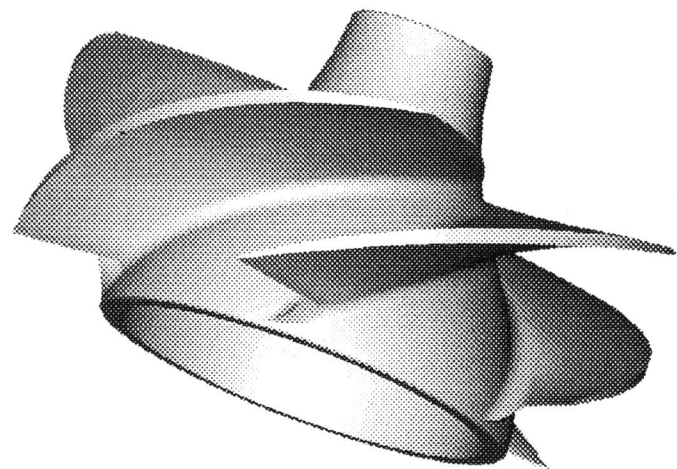

Figure 8.11. The Impeller.

Today these impellers (Figure 8.11) are manufactured by welding acid-proof steel blades and a body together. The body is turned from a pre casted part. The blades are made by the investment casting method using manually prepared steel blades as patterns in a epoxy tooling. After welding the weld seams will be grinded. Welding and grinding are disagreeable and very time consuming handwork because of the hardness of the material and the small and tight space between blades.

8.7.1 Tooling of Prototype and Digitising

At the begin of the project FFJet Ltd made a prototype model (Figure 8.12) of a impeller with a body and one blade. The diameter of the impeller was 243 mm and height 144 mm. This model was delivered with 2D-drawing of the body to HUT/Lahti Centre. Based on this drawing a parametric 3D-volume model from the

8.7 WATER JET IMPELLER

body was made. Because of the complex form of the blade it was digitised by a co-ordinate measuring machine from five different directions that was the number of directions required. All together about 10 000 co-ordinate points were collected.

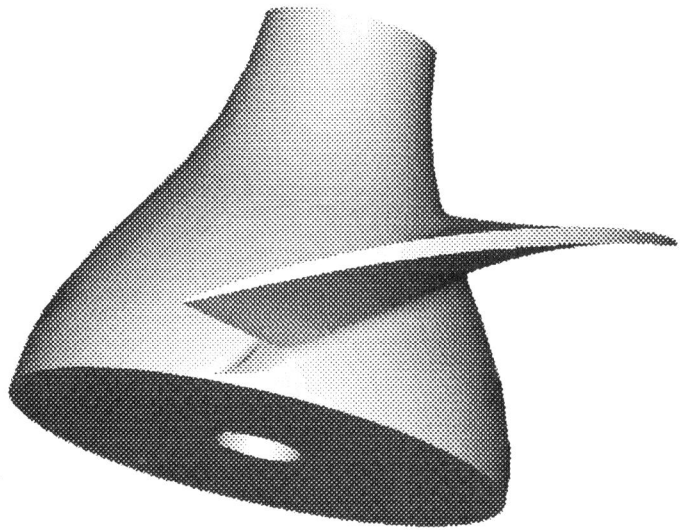

Figure 8.12. Body Pattern and the Blade Segment.

8.7.2 3D-CAD-Modelling

Based on these measured data a surface model of a blade was modelled. It consists of an upper and a lower surface and boundary surfaces. The modelling was done with Pro/Engineer 3D-CAD system and it's Scantool module which is meant for handling digitised data. The technology used in modelling phase was to extract contour curves from the point cloud. The surfaces were then modelled through this curves. After the surfaces were created the model was processed into solid model which was needed to export STL-file.

Next task was to design the wax patterns for investment casting. The impeller was devided into two pieces, a body pattern and a blade segment. The whole impeller consists of the body and five blade segments. The body pattern couldn't be divided in five segment because it's inside geometry form was not divisible by five. One blade pattern contained the actual blade and the skin of the body shell so that the whole impeller can be assembled by putting five blade segments around the body (Figure 8.13). The body pattern consists the rest of the body.

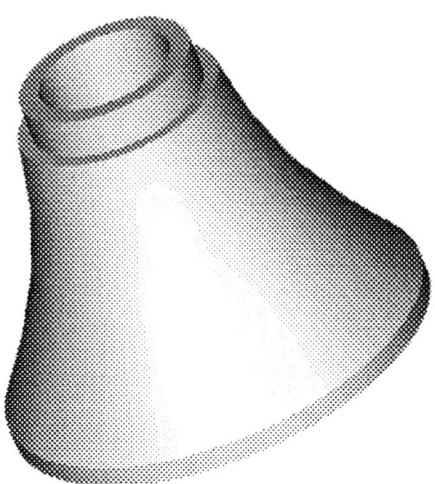

Figure 8.13. The Body Pattern.

8.7.3 Rapid Prototyping

First STL-files of the blade pattern and the body pattern were created. In STL-generation we used chord height 0.01 mm. The binary STL-file sizes were 1.7 MB (34 100 triangles) for the blade pattern and 1.4 MB (28 300 triangles) for the body pattern. STL-files were sent via ftp-connection to several RP-bureau's for an offer request. RP-models were ordered from SINTEF, Norway, which produced RP-models with Cubital machine. From SINTEF RP-models were sent to FFJet for inspection and finishing.

8.7.4 Soft Tooling and Investment Casting

From FFJet parts were sent to Sacotec for investment casting. Sacotec used RP-patterns to make the epoxy moulds. These moulds were used to prepare wax patterns. The final impeller wax patterns were made by joining 5 blade segments and one body pattern together (Figure 8.14). Totally 5 wax impeller patterns were made. The foundry used their standard wax material so the shell preparation and the casting process went trough with any problems. After investment casting the impellers were sent to FFJet Ltd for finishing, inspection and testing.

8.7 WATER JET IMPELLER

Figure 8.14. The Wax Pattern of the Impeller.

This project showed us that the process is very suitable to manufacture impeller. It decreases the product development and manufacturing time because the welding and the grinding phases are left away. There is ongoing work to develop this process further. The purpose of this work is to examine the dimension changes during process phases. Also an other digitising method, FARO-arm touch probe, will be tested. With this device it's possible to digitise whole impeller in one fastening. The goal is to optimise the process from digitising to 3D-CAD model and find also automatic functions for the 3D-CAD modelling.

HUT/Lahti Centre
Jukka Tuomi
Juhani Seppänen

9 PROCESS PLANNING AND RPT

The purpose of this Chapter is to investigate the possibility of automating tasks associated to process planning in order to increase the productivity of RP processes. The RP processes taken into consideration were those to which we had access within the Consortium. The results for this Chapter are restricted to guidelines and suggestions for further research.

As defined by Shah and Mantyla:
Process planning stands for a family of planning tasks that must be completed before a designed product can be manufactured.

This definition is certainly very broad as it includes almost everything related to manufacturing, from the selection of manufacturing technologies to the determination of individual process parameters and the resources required to carry out each individual step. Unfortunately, it seems to be impossible to address all these problems at once in order to arrive at an optimal process plan. In practice, either information is not available or it is not possible to control the entire manufacturing process, e.g. if some manufacturing steps are outsourced. Besides, some decision-making processes may be very difficult - or impossible - to capture in the form of a computer program. On the other hand, some tasks can be highly automated. This is the case, for instance, of NC code generation from feature-based solid models.

Instead of addressing the entire problem, a multi-level approach is taken. In this Chapter, we will consider the following levels:

1. Process planning (PP) for one individual RPT process
2. For process chains
3. PP for selecting suitable a manufacturing process or processes

Each of these levels will be explained in the sequel. Before doing so, we discuss differences and similarities between RPT and conventional manufacturing, trying to understand the essence of new problems from what is already known from older problems.

9.1 RPT VS CONVENTIONAL MANUFACTURING

RP is a significant departure from traditional manufacturing in many ways. Most striking, of course, is the fact that, generally speaking, material is added layer-by-layer and excess material is removed at a later stage. The building method eliminates the need for a process planner to check for collisions.

Adding material may be more elegant than removing it, but it does not imply in higher sophistication. Moving parts away from the working area and removing excess material must be done manually. Skill is needed to remove support structures attached to delicate features or melting away wax from narrow orifices. Polishing the part in order to eliminate staircase effects is an art and still far from being under control.

Another significant difference is the method chosen to transfer the geometry of the part. The most common method is using a faceted representation in a form called the STL format. Several other sources have described this format, and we will assume the reader is familiar with it. The consequence of this for a process planner is that the description of the part contains no features in the sense commonly attached to this term. Features likely holes and ribs are the entities used by a process planner to perform optimisations. If they are not given, they are extremely difficult to find and there is no guarantee that the relevant ones are actually found.

In the case of NC milling, a process planner has access to all parameters that control the cutting through well-defined file formats. Unlike RP processes, the architecture of a milling machine is open. Specifying the building parameters for an RP process must be done via vendor-supplied software tools. This imposes practical limitations for optimising operations for individual needs and applications.

The advent of RPT puts additional constraints on data preparation. Preparing NC Tool Paths has always been subject to improvements over the years, but compared to RPT, data preparation times are much longer. Long delays are not acceptable in RPT; common data preparation times are below 2 hours. Relatively speaking, a skilled operator is needed for milling; in RPT, a ``push-button" or ``black-box" approach is preferred, i.e. it usually up to software tools to assign and select optimal parameters and procedures.

9.2 PROCESS PLANNING FOR INDIVIDUAL RPT PROCESSES

It would be far too ambitious to analyse in-depth each RPT process. Instead, we will address common problems and provide details only in selected cases. The boundaries of the process must be defined. In this Section, a process includes the software tools delivered with the equipment, the equipment itself, and post-processing activities such as removing support structures and polishing.

At this level, two main questions must be addressed:

1. Can the part be build using a particular process?
2. If so, how should it be build, how much will it cost and how long will it take?

The most severe bottlenecks we have seen are related to data preparation and post-processing. Uncertainties in delivery times are usually caused by data transfer and preparation. If the model is not correct, or it cannot easily be loaded into the software programs for further processing, then it is not possible to give accurate quotation to the user. As for post-processing, the most significant problems are related to the elimination of the staircase effect through polishing without affecting accuracy. Removal of excess material can pose problems as well.

Each process imposes several constraints. The most obvious is the maximum size of the working space. This limitation can be overcome by splitting the part in pieces, and putting them back together later, provided the process is accurate enough and the geometry allows it. The state-of-the-art regarding this problem is the good judgement of a human operator coupled with suitable software tools to carry out the splitting. The Solid Ground Curing (SGC) process is delivered with most of the necessary tools, but other processes must resort to third-party software vendors.

The Laminated Object Manufacturing (LOM) process has a sub-optimal hatching strategy. Unlike other processes, the material that must be removed from the layer is hatched. This material is later removed by mechanical forces increasing the possibility that the part is damaged. By contrast, surrounding wax in a SGC process is melted away, and excess resin in an SLA drips away. Different hatching strategies could overcome some of these problems in addition to improved building speed.

A basic operation any process planner would need to perform is selecting a building orientation for the part. Currently, this is done by the operator using information supplied by the user and it is not regarded as a significant problem. The information consists of surface finish characteristics needed in the final part and it may be supplied in different ways. Addressing this problem using automated tools may be of more interest in the future when the productivity required reaches much higher levels than today.

The SGC and LOM processes permit that parts be nested since support structures are not needed. Again, nesting of parts is done by the operator and it is not a significant problem if suitable tools are available to simplify the task. For instance, checking for interference's (or part intersections) is very important. Automatic tools, at this time, do offer significant productivity improvements to these processes.

9.3 PROCESS PLANNING FOR PROCESS CHAINS

It is relatively recent that the accuracy of RPT processes has reached good levels. Today, it a model can be split and then combined without affecting accuracy. Several years after the introduction of RPT process to the market, pieces manufactured separately could not be combined because they did not fit together.

Due to accuracy improvements, part made via RPT can be used as masters in a process chain. The term process chain refers to when one or more processes are used to manufacture a part. For instance, a master may be manufactured using Quickcast and used with vacuum casting to obtain a silicon rubber mould. The mould may be filled with low-temperature melting materials to produce several copies of the part. This particular technique is widely used nowadays.

The challenge of a process planner at this level is to take into account the characteristics of the entire chain. The starting point may be the geometry of the part or the mould. If the geometry of the part is given, deriving the geometry of the mould is usually the major bottleneck. Even verifying if the geometry satisfies the constraints of the chain can be difficult, error-prone, or even impossible. In the case of tooling, parting lines, parting surfaces, and draft angles need to be considered. These topics provide plenty of research problems and will not be addressed here.

9.4 PROCESS PLANNING FOR SELECTING A SUITABLE MANUFACTURING PROCESS OR CHAIN

Given the ever increasing number of RP processes on the market, the question arises on how to choose which process is most suitable for a given geometry. If one does not restrict oneself to RPT processes alone, one could address equally

9.4 PROCESS PLANNING FOR SELECTING A SUITABLE

well the problem of choosing between an RPT process and milling techniques. Even further, a set of processes for a given geometry may be the optimal solution.

The need for such tools, at this time, can be questioned. The pace at which the technology is evolving is great and it would be difficult to keep knowledge concerning a given RPT process accurate and up-to-date. Besides,

the capabilities of a given process depends very much on who is operating the equipment, and this information may can only be gathered and codified under very special conditions. Optimal solutions in this setting are often local; for instance, milling may be attractive to one user simply because the equipment is in-house. Finally, the number of users that would benefit from such tools is, most likely, to be relatively small.

A tool that allows a user to experiment with different alternatives in order to search for a viable solution will be attractive in the future.